CW00456357

ECONOMIC PRIORITIES FOR A LABOUR GOVERNMENT

Economic Priorities for a Labour Government

Roy Hattersley
Shadow Chancellor of the Exchequer
Deputy Leader of the Labour Party

Edited and introduced by
Doug Jones
Economic Adviser to Roy Hattersley

**MACMILLAN
PRESS**

First published 1987

Published by
THE MACMILLAN PRESS LTD
Houndmills, Basingstoke, Hampshire RG21 2XS
and London
Companies and representatives
throughout the world

Typeset by Wessex Typesetters
(Division of The Eastern Press Ltd)
Frome, Somerset

Printed in Great Britain by
Anchor Brendon Ltd
Tiptree, Essex

British Library Cataloguing in Publication Data
Hattersley, Roy
Economic priorities for a labour
government.
1. Labour Party (*Great Britain*)   2. Great
Britain——Economic policy——1945–
I. Title   II. Jones, Doug
330.941'0858   HC256.6
ISBN 0–333–44727–1 (hardcover)
ISBN 0–333–44728–X (paperback)

To Nasreen Rahman

Contents

Acknowledgements

This book is based upon the economic speeches given by Roy Hattersley between February 1984 and February 1987. Special thanks are due to Roy's outside advisers for their help: Tony Atkinson, David Currie, Gavyn Davies, John Hills, Bill McKenzie, David Metcalf, Henry Neuburger, Paul Ormerod, Maurice Peston, Dennis Turner and Charles Williams. Within Roy's office David Hill and I helped with the preparation of the speeches on which this book is based.

Since most of those acknowledged are economists, no two of them will agree with all of the views expressed, or indeed about anything else. Responsibility for the views expressed in Chapters 2–16 therefore rests with Roy Hattersley, whilst responsibility for the introductory chapter and the editing is mine alone.

On occasion Justin Ash, Seb Berry, Frankie Blagden, William Brown, Bernard Donaghue, Alan Hughes and Nasreen Rahman have also given assistance or carried out research. Roy's Secretary, Joyce Farrell typed most of the speeches originally and retyped many of them for this book. Thanks go also to Mavis Reed, Audrey Channon and June Phipps for typing the rest of the chapters in the space of only ten days.

Mike Campbell, David Currie, David Hill, Maurice Peston and Dennis Turner speedily read the manuscript in draft form at very short notice and offered valuable suggestions for improvement, while Keith Povey and Barbara Docherty ensured swift yet efficient copy-editing and proof-reading.

The author and publishers would like to thank the following for permission to reproduce copyright material: *Marxism Today*, October 1985; *Tribune*, 10 May 1985; *Account*, 18 July 1985; *Sunday Times*, 16 December 1984; *Financial Times*, 4 July 1986, 20 November 1985; *The Economist*, 7 December 1985; *The Independent*, January 1987; the Institute of Fiscal Studies, *Public Finances in Perspective*, Report No. 8, February 1984; the CBI, *Change to Succeed*, 1985; the Institute Of Personnel Management, *Practical Participation and Involvement*, Vol. 5, *Pay And Benefits*, 1982; the Institute of Fiscal Studies, *Fiscal Studies*, Vol. 6, February 1985; Greenwell Montagu Research, *The Labour Party's Emerging*

Economic Strategy, May 1986; Wheatsheaf Books Ltd, R. H. Tauney, *The Acquisitive Society*, 1982; André Deutch, S. Plender, *That's The Way The Money Goes*, 1982; Allen & Unwin, R. H. Tauney, *The Radical Tradition*, 1966; Virago, B. Webb, *The Diaries 1924–43*, Vol. 4, 1985.

DOUG JONES

1 Introduction: The Development of a New Economic Programme

Doug Jones

THE INHERITANCE

In June 1983, the headline total for unemployment was two million more than when the Conservatives were elected in May 1979. Yet one opinion poll at the time of the 1983 election showed that the electorate believed the Conservatives to have a more convincing policy to tackle unemployment than Labour. This was the true measure of the depths to which the Labour Party had sunk.

There were many reasons for Labour's defeat in 1983, not least internal divisions and the formation of the SDP. These enabled the Tory Party to increase its Parliamentary majority despite a fall in its share of the national vote. But these are not the only reasons for the failure of Labour's economic policy to convince the electorate. As Roy Hattersley said:

> The people of Britain looked at our economic policy, admired our compassion but doubted our capacity [COHSE Meeting, St Albans, 8 January 1985].*

The problems were intrinsic to the Alternative Economic Strategy. The roots of this policy can be traced back to the early 1970s when it was developed partly as a reaction to the experience of the Wilson Governments in the 1960s. In the 1980s it received a new lease of life, again as a reaction to the experience of Labour in office. A policy that had been developed originally for a pre-recession, pre-monetarist world did not pay enough attention to a future Labour Government's malign economic and political inheritance from the Thatcher Government. The nature of the economic task had been charged by the acceleration of the decline

---

* Please note that all quotations and references are to speeches or interviews given by Roy Hattersley unless otherwise indicated.

of manufacturing industry and the advent and subsequent decline of North Sea oil production. The nature of the political task had been changed by the alteration of people's attitudes to public ownership, taxation, planning, borrowing and above all the role of Government. Even leaving aside the legacy from Mrs Thatcher there can be no going back to the policies practised and the alternatives proposed in the 1960s and 1970s, not least because of the constraints imposed by the new international economic environment. Quitting the EEC is no longer an option. There has been continued growth in the power of multinational corporations. International currency movements are now dominated by speculative private capital flows rather than by trade in goods and services. Import penetration and the proportion of production dependent on international trade have both increased in the UK. And the international consensus in favour of co-operation and expansion has been destroyed. Together these have required a rethinking of the options available to a country determined to tackle unemployment. Policy after 1983 not only had to be repackaged, it had to be replaced.

UNEMPLOYMENT

Roy Hattersley was elected Deputy Leader of the Labour Party in September 1983. He was given the task of re-establishing the credibility of Labour's economic policy when Neil Kinnock appointed him as Shadow Chancellor of the Exchequer in November 1983. The mainspring of Hattersley's approach to his portfolio was summed up in his speech to the 1984 Labour Party Conference:

> It is the moral duty of the next Labour Government to put Britain back to work ... We can remedy the callous incompetence of eight or nine years of Thatcherism, but we cannot do it overnight. And we can only do it if we win the election. We will not shock or shame Mrs Thatcher into reducing the dole queues. For her unemployment is an essential element of economic policy. It emasculates the Unions and it depresses wages ... We have a duty to the unemployed first to win the election and then to put them back to work. If, through

self-interest or self-indulgence, timidity or factionalism, we fail to achieve our objective, we will not be forgiven. Nor will we deserve to be forgiven [Party Conference, Blackpool, 4 October 1984].

Hattersley explicitly rejects the Two Nations approach of the Conservatives exemplified by Lord David Young's statement that:

This country has never had so good a time as it has today . . . We've never had it so good for the 87 per cent of us who are working [Lord Young, TV AM, May 1986].

Hattersley is convinced that:

In Ministers' minds, the nation has been divided into two distinct groups – the men and women whose votes can be captured for Conservatives and those votes and, therefore, interests have been written off. Principle amongst the candidates for wilful neglect are the 3½ million unemployed (who incidentally will receive no tax cuts at all). The Government now believes that if unemployment can be stabilised at about its present level, the men and women now in work will no longer fear for themselves or care about their out of work neighbours. The money which might have been used to put Britain back to work is to be used to buy votes [Birmingham, 8 December 1985].

The Tories therefore try to define economic success in a way that excludes reference to the appalling levels of unemployment that we have in Britain. That is unacceptable for:

A definition of recovery which does not include putting Britain back to work is not a definition that can be acceptable in a civilised society [Party Conference, Blackpool, 4 October 1984].

Labour's policy is jobs first. (See Ch. 2.) But to put that into practice required Labour to devise a strategy to get elected:

The agreement to that priority (to reduce unemployment) requires us to do more than luxuriate in the good intention of our official policy . . . Sympathy with the men and women in the dole queues is not an adequate substitute for a programme constructed with sufficient intellectual rigour to ensure that we begin to put them back to work. This is no time for well-meaning sentimentalists who first call for a cut in unemployment and then vote for policies which – though desirable in themselves – make a substantial reduction impossible [Aneurin Bevan Memorial Lecture, Redditch, 14 October 1984].

Hattersley and his advisers believed that one of the reasons for Labour's failure to convince the electorate of the practicality of its anti-unemployment policy lay in the selection of a target to reduce unemployment from over three million to one million. The widespread opinion that the one million target was unrealistic possibly encouraged the belief that nothing could be done about unemployment. Arguments centred on the one million target and the reliability of the computer model runs that were supposed to demonstrate its feasibility. The question of whether or not it was possible to reduce unemployment was lost. The Conservatives had successfully downgraded the expectations of what Governments could achieve. 'There is no alternative' was one of the Tories more widely accepted economic myths. Its confident assertion was embodied in the crude but superficially appealing Medium-Term Financial Strategy. (See Ch. 3.) Against this background, and given the Labour Party's disorganised state, Labour's economic policy was not politically credible:

During the ten years before our defeat in 1979 – whatever the real merits of our programmes and policy – Labour was increasingly portrayed and increasingly regarded as committed to theoretical (and unworkable) solutions to the real problems of the British economy. At the 1979 election, the new Conservatism of Margaret Thatcher was believed to have found a near infallible solution to our economic problems. The nation had come to believe that no Government could beneficially play a direct part in the operation of the economy. Salvation was to come through *laissez-faire* [Margaret Gibb Memorial Lecture, Newcastle, 30 March 1985].

The task of Labour was to switch the argument from a debate about whether or not the million unemployment target was feasible back to a debate about whether it was possible for Governments to reduce unemployment at all. In early 1984 a decision was taken deliberately to downgrade Labour's claims of what could be achieved by setting out the constraints that would face an incoming Labour Government:

> If we promise to do everything or pretend that we can achieve our objectives easily or quickly, we will end up doing nothing, for the voters will not take us seriously giving us the chance to put Britain back to work. I do not intend that the next Labour Government like our French comrades should begin with 2 years of unrealistic agreement to every attractive proposition and end with 2 years of near bankruptcy, deepening deflation, increasing disillusionment among our supporters and mounting despair with the voters [AEUW Conference, Eastbourne, 22 April 1985].

Pointing out the constraints and decreasing the size of the target for the reduction in unemployment was not a callous disregard of the unemployed. The ambition to maximise the reduction in unemployment remains undiminished. Of course if the target proves easy to hit then it will be exceeded. But the reduction of unemployment does not come about through targets set in opposition. It comes about through action, through building up a body of opinion in favour, and through power in Government. This happens only if people are given confidence that something can be done. And to do that it is necessary to take account of the depressed state of their expectations:

> My entire life in the Labour Party has convinced me that we ought not to be a socialist Sunday school, or a sixth form debating society. Our object is to become the Government of the country. And therefore I'm very sceptical about people who say, 'You're only doing this to win votes'. Therefore I don't for a moment step back from the allegation or compliment, or whatever you care to call it. I want to make the Labour Party the head of a great national consensus which produces a majority Government [*Marxism Today*, October 1985].

Having shown that Labour recognised the constraints on reducing unemployment, the next plan was to demonstrate that even within the Government's own framework there was scope to take measures to reduce unemployment. In preparing the responses to the 1984 and 1985 budgets:

> We based our spending proposals on what could have been

done within the Government's own parameters. Eighteen months ago [i.e., in 1984] there was much less agreement that Governments could do something to reduce unemployment. By working within broad Tory parameters, and concentrating the argument on whether tax cuts or public expenditure was best for creating jobs, we established the idea that a cut in unemployment was possible. The debate now concerns not whether we can create jobs, but how many jobs can be created and what is the best way to generate employment. There is now a Labour led consensus that we need public capital investment as part of a package to reduce unemployment [Private paper presented to Shadow Cabinet, 12 February 1986].

PUBLIC EXPENDITURE VERSUS TAX CUTS

Hattersley regards the decision taken to campaign for public expenditure – particularly public investment expenditure – rather than tax cuts as one of the most influential in helping turn the economic debate in Labour's favour. The Government could not demand where the money would come from for they, themselves, had said that money was available for tax cuts and decreases in borrowing. The debate was therefore over the use of spare resources. Labour demanded they be used for public expenditure as this was a more effective means to reduce unemployment than tax cuts. Moreover, a series of reports from the National Economic Development Office, the Department of the Environment and the Audit Commission have all shown a serious backlog of infrastructure maintenance and repair work. That work must be carried out if the cost is not to escalate in future years. Contrary to Government propaganda, there is plenty of necessary work in the public sector. In seeking to tackle unemployment, Labour was not just advocating 'makework' schemes of little benefit to the economy as a whole:

> The social, economic and political advantage of our proposals is that they will finance substantial improvements in health, education, environment and local Government programmes as well as reducing unemployment [Private paper presented to Shadow Cabinet, 17 July 1986].

Almost every serious commentator, academic economist and

econometric model (including the Treasury's own) supported Labour's contention that the Government was on weak ground in arguing that tax cuts were the most effective way to reduce unemployment (see Chapter 4). Labour could present itself at the head of a consensus that also included many Conservative and Alliance MPs, the Trade Unions, the Bishops, much business opinion and most Tory newspapers. For the first time since well before the 1983 election the economic battle was now being fought on ground of Labour's choosing with the Tory Government on the defensive:

> The idea of lower unemployment no longer seemed an impractical ideal [COHSE Meeting, St Albans, 8 January 1985].

It did not matter for Party purposes in 1984 and 1985 that some Liberal, Tory or SDP MPs echoed Labour policies, for that only helped to reinforce the view that it was the Government, not the Labour Party, that was acting outside the consensus.

It is possible to gauge the extent to which this approach has worked. The Government's own propaganda has shifted from vitriolic attacks on public expenditure to attempts to take credit for increases in public expenditure, even though many of these increases have been due to their failure to hit pre-announced policy targets for cuts. This has even gone so far as to them erecting hoardings drawing attention to their responsibility for capital projects – a trick they borrowed from the socialist Greater London Council. The final admission that the Government was losing the ideological battle over public expenditure was the sudden U-turn announced in the 1986 Autumn Statement in which they announced a £4.7 billion pre-election boost to spending.

In moving from a position of 'public expenditure bad, public expenditure cuts good' to a position of 'public expenditure good, public expenditure cuts bad' the former intellectual clarity and consistency of Tory policy has been lost. They have been forced to concede the ideological and intellectual ground to Labour over the issue of public expenditure. And there is not much likelihood that they will be able to convince the general public that their public expenditure policies are superior to those of Labour. They spent four years in opposition and six years in Government arguing for cuts in public expenditure. This is an easier case for a

Conservative to put convincingly because this is what people expect to hear from Conservatives. In George Orwell's *Animal Farm*, when the pigs began to chant 'two legs good, four legs bad' there was an uneasy feeling that left the other animals not wholly convinced. Was it just their faulty memories or had the pigs in the mists of time led them to power on the back of the slogan 'four legs good, two legs bad'?

The extent of the ideological difficulties faced by the Tories is illustrated by the British social attitudes survey. This shows that the proportion of the population wanting to increase taxes and spend more on health, education and social benefits increased from 32 per cent in 1983 to 45 per cent in 1985. Those advocating no change fell from 54 per cent to 43 per cent. And those wanting to cut taxes and spend less fell to only 6 per cent.

TAXATION, REDISTRIBUTION AND EQUALITY

The Conservatives are now stuck in the position of trying to deliver tax cuts when politically there is no demand for them. Perhaps the determination to cut taxes lies in part in their embarrassment at having increased – not cut – the tax burden on most taxpayers. In fact, they have cut the taxes only of the best off. The top 5 per cent of taxpayers and receivers of capital income, gains and transfers have had annual tax cuts of well over £3.6 billion:

> The Chancellor has attempted to justify this reduction by claiming that it provides added incentive for those at the top of the income scale. Indeed he has already argued that a reduction in tax rates actually increases the tax income from those on the highest income. This is palpable nonsense. Recent increases in the percentage of revenue collected from those in the highest tax brackets are not the results of lower marginal rates. They are the product of a widening divergence between the primary earnings of the rich and the primary earnings of the rest – a divergence which has little or nothing to do with the incentive effect of lower tax rates. [According to the Treasury, the earnings of the top 10 per cent of men rose seven times as fast under the Conservative Government as the earnings of the bottom 10 per cent.] It was not lower tax rates that prompted

the Chairman of recently privatised industries to increase their salaries . . . The massive salaries now paid in the City are in no way related to tax cuts. To justify lower taxes as a way to ensure that the rich help the poor is transparent hypocrisy – greed dressed up to look like benevolence [International Equity Dealers, London, 15 January 1987].

The scale of tax cuts to the richest 5 per cent enabled Labour to propose that quite substantial improvements in pensions, child benefit and long-term supplementary benefit for the long-term unemployed could be made without raising taxes on the vast majority of tax payers (see Chapter 4). This redistribution was first proposed in 1984 and repeated in subsequent years.

Hattersley's commitment to redistribution and equality has undoubtedly been one of the most controversial aspects of his proposals. In September 1985, six newspaper editorials all attacked his plans on the same day. Two demanded his replacement – presumably on the grounds that prospective socialist Chancellors should not actually advocate reductions in inequality. Perhaps the response of the national newspapers reflected the fact that the journalists who write for them are themselves amongst the 5 per cent of the population who have been the beneficiaries of Mrs Thatcher's largesse. In order to try to discredit Hattersley's proposals some newspapers ran stories claiming that he proposed to raise taxes on middle-income couples whose joint income was over £20 000 – for example a teacher married to a nurse. This was despite the fact that Hattersley has consistently advocated independent taxation for men and women which would make such joint taxation impossible.

Another occasion upon which Hattersley's remarks were subject to major distortion was his supposed references to the 'bloody rich'. He was asked by *Tribune*: 'Do you see a massive need to take back the money that Margaret Thatcher gave to the rich in tax reductions?' He replied:

Yes I do. I see it as a moral necessity as well as an economic necessity. That money is necessary to fund the social programme, the poverty programme. But I also find it offensive to live in a society where the rich have had tax cuts and the poor now pay a greater percentage of their earnings in taxes . . .

I call the rich the top 15% who earn £20 000 a year or more. They may not all be *very* rich but, compared with the constituents that I represent, they are bloody rich. Its a different world they live in [*Tribune*, 10 May 1985].

It is worth recalling that Birmingham Sparkbrook (Hattersley's constituency) is one of the poorest parts of Britain with almost 50 per cent male unemployment in one of its three wards.

Hattersley has constantly stressed the issue of equality in his speeches whether they have been about domestic or international and Third World issues (see Chapter 15). Indeed he has drawn a parallel between the Thatcher Government's attitude to domestic and foreign problems:

The truth is that the poorest parts of the world are still subsidising the richest. The parallel with what is happening in Britain is tragically clear. Here the poor pay higher taxes, are paid less, and suffer deteriorating public services in order that the Government can give £3.6 bn a year to the highest 5% in tax reliefs. The values which characterise that domestic policy – greed, complacency and self-interest – are the principles which also guide the Conservative approach to international problems [Overseas Development Institute, London, 10 June 1986].

Hattersley has also set out what there is for women within his approach to equality:

There are two things in it for women. I don't believe that those groups within the population, minorities or a majority which are at present disadvantaged, are likely to have those disadvantages ended during a period of recession. If we can move the economy forward we are more likely to provide employment opportunities and facilities for women. Secondly, though it won't be my responsibility directly, I hope that in the area of women and also ethnic minorities we are going to do the two things that socialism requires us to do in our pursuit of equality. One is to provide the formal rights – for example, rights for women to be employed in certain occupations which still, covertly if not overtly, discriminate against them. But equally, too, we are going to provide the facilities which enable the previously disadvantaged groups to take advantage of their new rights. It's no good coming to my constituency and saying that we are going to insist that women who apply for certain jobs are given a fair chance of getting them if there aren't facilities which enable the women to go to work – there's somebody looking after their kids, they've got shops open at different times etc.

What I've said, for instance, about an assault on low pay – I am a believer in a statutory minimum wage – will do a great deal to assist women. I don't take the view that a statutory minimum wage will prevent women from working. I take quite the opposite view [*Marxism Today*, October 1985].

He is also an advocate of public sector contract compliance which promotes equal opportunities and of a rapid move to independent taxation for men and women. He has helped shift the Party's position on independent taxation so that not all of the proceeds from the abolition of the married man's allowance are to be used to raise child benefit. Such a move would have involved significant transfers of income from poorer, childless, working-class couples to better-off, middle-class couples with children. The move to independent taxation is now part of a package of reforms including child benefit increases which ensures income protection or improvement for the less well off. The Party's policy now enhances both income and sexual equality and this should smooth its path to implementation after the election. This is consistent with Hattersley's more traditional view of sexual inequality which he sees as being part of the problem of inequality in general rather than as an issue to be analysed separately.

The pursuit of equality is a concept that constantly appears in his speeches, for it forms part of his ideological frame of reference.

I believe that socialism is essentially about freedom, and the only way we can become genuinely free is to become more equal. The material equality which I want to promote is a means to allowing more people to have freedom, which is the ultimate object of a socialist society. I would like to see us measure all our policies against that aim. I'm writing a book [*Choose Freedom*, published in 1987] which says that what's been wrong with the Labour Party in the recent past is that we've never defined what our aim is. Pragmatism has become a major socialist virtue. Yet it hasn't prevented us from receiving all the assaults which pragmatism was supposed to protect us from and it's stopped us from measuring our policies against anything worthwhile. Equality and freedom – two things which I don't think can be distinguished – are the ultimate aim of my socialism. A reduction in unemployment, while that is the first essential step to making us a slightly more equal society, since unemployment produces the most desperate poverty and bequeaths it to future generations, must be seen as part of the ultimate objective [*Marxism Today*, October 1985].

The reasons tax cuts – especially tax cuts confined to the rich – have not had the popular appeal that the Conservatives and their newspapers hoped are twofold. First, as has been the case with all post-war Governments with the exception of the first Thatcher administration the real incomes of significant groups of people in work have risen. And the higher up the income scale the greater has been the increase. They do not need tax cuts to compensate for poor pre-tax wages.

Second, as people's incomes go up they tend to want to spend a higher proportion on services. These services include those that in Britain are primarily provided by the public sector – education and health. State education is provided to 94 per cent of children and the NHS is the sole source of health care for 85 per cent of the population. And a large part of the population uses public transport. As people's incomes rise they want better public provision in these areas – the improved services that tax cuts cannot buy. The Conservatives are perceived to have cut back or not to care about public provision. The entire Cabinet has preferred private education for its children and Mrs Thatcher makes a public virtue of not travelling by rail and having her health ailments treated privately. The real failure of Thatcherism has been its inability significantly to roll back state provision in these areas, and with it she has failed to roll back the popularity of public expenditure.

FISCAL FRAMEWORK

Consistent with the decision to concentrate extra spending or borrowing on policies which generate reductions in unemployment there has been a constant emphasis on a firm financial framework for Labour policy:

We shall concentrate the nation's resources on the greatest single challenge and the greatest single crisis which now confronts us – the crisis of unemployment. It is possible to create something like one million jobs in about two years. But to achieve that essential aim, the funds we have available must be used, almost exclusively, for that purpose. We do not propose to be sidetracked from our primary obligation.

The days have gone when we could hope to achieve all our ambitions in the life-time of a single parliament. It is necessary for us to fix our clear priorities and to insist that all other tasks and targets take second place. That is what we propose as the central feature of the Labour Government's economic policy [TSSA Conference, Bournemouth, 13 May 1986].

And, addressing his Shadow Cabinet colleagues in July 1986 Hattersley said:

In the past the Labour Party in opposition has done itself much damage by its attitudes towards and its promises about public expenditure. In the preparation for previous elections we have almost always committed ourselves to more public spending than the electorate thought credible and the economy could reasonably bear. During the last three years we have largely managed to avoid such self-inflicted wounds. It is vital that we continue to do so – both in order to ensure the election of a majority Labour Government and to enable that Government to achieve its major policy priorities.

A firm line on expenditure was not taken for reasons of political machismo:

I don't see myself as the natural heir to Stafford Cripps; I'm not going to offer five years of austerity [*Tribune*, 10 May 1985].

It is true that a tough stance helped make Labour's position stronger with a sceptical electorate but its main purpose was to enable the Party to promise something substantial on the employment front.

It was because Labour had set out a firm framework that an attempt by John MacGregor, Chief Secretary to the Treasury, to caricature Labour's proposals as involving massive increases in public expenditure, could find no takers amongst serious journalists or outside bodies such as the Institute of Fiscal Studies and the National Institute for Economic and Social Research (see Chapter 4).

Indeed if Hattersley's redistributive tax plans created the greatest outcry in the press then his proposals for reform in the way Labour approaches public borrowing and assess the efficiency of public expenditure have gained him some of the most favourable comment (see Chapters 4 and 5). These proposals included the use of a public sector balance sheet, zero based budgeting, efficiency measures alongside cash limits and the replacement of the Public Sector Borrowing Requirement.

> I don't think we want to play these absurd Public Sector Borrowing Requirement games. The 'Public Sector Borrowing Requirement' is not a phrase I ever intend to use when I am Chancellor. We are going to have proper and prudent control of public borrowing, but the nonsense about public sector prices (which have been forced up as a means of back door taxation), like the nonsense about selling public sector assets, like the nonsense about public sector investment, is partly the result of a stupid PSBR definition [*Tribune*, 10 May 1985].

The importance of fiscal reform is that it ensures that if a government does run into difficulties it is easier to maintain priority within expenditure for those areas most essential for the long-term health of the economy – investment, industry and employment. Too often in the past cuts have been made in those areas of expenditure which do most damage to industry and employment. On other occasions sensible proposals for expenditure have been dropped for no other reason than political prejudice.

> The amount of the national budget which can be taken up by State spending is not an absolute. One of the reasons I fell out with Roy Jenkins to whom I used to be politically close, was a speech of his in which he claimed a free society could not support more than 40% of GNP being in the hands of the State [*Account*, 18 July 1985].

The need to stick to priorities in expenditure not only applies to the allocation of resources in the public sector but also to questions such as pay. Some advisers argued that on economic grounds, some of Labour's targets would be easier to hit if the Party had a formal incomes policy. The experience of the 1974–9 incomes policy, which towards the end of office Hattersley was largely responsible for running, has lead him to rule out such a formal policy, although he still emphasises the need to discuss pay with both sides of industry.

It seems to me quite extraordinary that free collective bargaining, which is a product of free market capitalism and embodies most of the disadvantages of that system, has become a canon of socialist belief. An agreement on incomes should not be a technique for heaping the burden of economic recovery on the backs of the workers. It is right in itself and I propose to argue for it in that language [Aneurin Bevan Memorial Lecture, Redditch, 14 October 1984].

I see the need for an agreement with the Trade Unions on pay, but then I see the need for an agreement with the Trades Unions on everything. What I said . . . was not simply 'let us talk about pay', it was 'let us talk about investment, let us talk about regional policy, let us talk about exchange rates, let us talk about exchange control, let us talk about taxation' [*Tribune*, 10 May 1985].

During the 1985 Trade Union Conference round Hattersley constantly reiterated the same message. The first call on resources had to be the unemployed, the second low paid and the poor, and the third, everyone else (see Chapter 2):

The truth is – it was one of the factors which determined the outcome of the last General Election – that workers in continuous employment who earn above average wages have not done badly under the Conservatives. It is the lower paid and the unemployed who have suffered and we cannot allow some mistaken view that the better off have to make up for years of restraint, to prejudice the work we have to do for the two really disadvantaged groups [Aneurin Bevan Memorial Lecture, 14 October 1984].

Let me make it clear that I am not saying [to the Unions] that if you scratch our backs we will scratch yours. I can think of nothing more disastrous either for the next Labour Government or for the Trade Union movement than a bargain which, on the one hand, requires the Government to introduce policies which it knows to be wrong and in return expects the

Trade Unions to accept laws which they regard as undesirable. I am not asking you to swallow a bitter pill which, in some devious and complicated way, the next Labour Government will sweeten. What I propose is that we get together to discuss and determine policies which we mutually agree are in the National interest . . .

The choice lies very much with the Trade Unions. I repeat the promise that I made to the Labour Party Conference. I have no intention of presiding over a statutory Incomes Policy nor of managing an Incomes Policy which although not statutory in form is coercion in fact. I have been over both of these courses before and I do not propose to create hurdles over which the next Labour Government will fall. I do however intend to offer the Trade Union movement the figures that confirm the facts. If we come to agreement about every aspect of our economic policy, we will be able to achieve our aims much more quickly – particularly our principal aim of reduced unemployment. I say to you, as it is my duty to say to you, that between us we have to choose how fast we move towards our goals. The choice will be as much yours as mine. But it is a choice that we have to make [AEUW Conference, Eastbourne, 22 May 1985].

The deliberate repetition that responsibility for a reduction in unemployment rested as much with the Trade Unions as with the Labour Party in Government marked a change of tack from that pursued by earlier Labour Governments. There is now far more emphasis on partnership, with responsibilities on both sides of the Labour movement. Although generally accepted, this approach has not been unanimously endorsed by every Trade Union leader. Whilst accepting the importance of pay, one said that they would find it easier if a Labour Government simply imposed a pay policy on them once the election was over.

In discussing incomes, the pay cutting and profit sharing approach of the Government has obviously been explicitly rejected. Instead, in order to protect the lowest paid a statutory minimum wage has been proposed (see Chapter 14):

We do not have to choose between decent pay and full employment. Low wages are no guarantee of full employment. Indeed, it is the low paid who are most likely to become unemployed . . .

A statutory minimum wage is not a Trojan Horse for a statutory incomes policy. That is not on the agenda of the next Labour Government. But, with or without a minimum wage, we are going to discuss money, wages . . . Indeed, for a low pay strategy to work, we need the active co-operation of Trade Unions. For, if we stick to the old patterns and the old conventions, all we will achieve is the same level of poverty at a higher level of inflation. The result would be the same disparities in wealth and income and a slower advance towards our primary objective of putting Britain back to work [Party Conference, Blackpool, 2 October 1986].

THE EXCHANGE RATE

Redistribution of income and reduction in unemployment have been two of Hattersley's main themes. The third has been the need to revive manufacturing industry in order to fill the gap left in the balance of payments as oil runs out (see Chapter 7). In 1985 oil revenues peaked. We have now moved back into balance of payments current account deficit for the first time since before oil came fully on stream. In the meantime a £5 billion surplus on manufactured trade in 1978 is now predicted by the Government to be a £7.5 billion deficit in 1987. The run down of industry has been the major source of unemployment since 1979 (two million jobs have been lost). And unless it can be revived, the balance of payments will act as the most severe constraint on Labour's ambitions to generate growth and secure full employment. That has required Hattersley to take a view on the exchange rate and propose a modern new replacement for old style statutory exchange controls (Chapter 6).

There can be little doubt that the external value of sterling, particularly against the dollar, is still seen as a national virility symbol. Efforts to prevent its devaluation between 1964 and 1967 meant that the first Wilson Government wasted its first three years in office and helped to reinforce the UK's continuing relative economic decline. And the proposal before the 1983 election to devalue sterling by 30 per cent was one of the factors said to have undermined the credibility of Labour's economic policy. In fact, that scale of depreciation has been more than 'achieved' by the Conservatives since the election. The annual sterling crises in early 1984, early 1985, and early 1986 did much to undermine confidence in the Government's ability to handle the economy – particularly when sterling almost dropped to parity with the dollar in Spring 1985. Indeed under the Conservatives the annual sterling difficulties have become almost as predictable as the January sales. The January 1987 problems which saw record lows against the Deutschmark, despite the highest real UK interest rates on record, went largely unnoticed by the general public. Unlike the dollar rate, the Deutschmark rate is not announced on the news each day. Even though the sterling–Deutschmark exchange rate is of equal if not superior economic importance, it is the sterling–dollar exchange rate that has most political impact. The regularity of the annual sterling depreciations has led Hattersley – somewhat tongue in cheek – to identify a new economic cycle to sit alongside the Kondratieff long cycles, the business cycles and the electoral cycles. In March 1986, he published his new theory:

The 'Lawson cycle' begins before Christmas with bragging and boasting concerning what will appear in the March Budget. Sometimes the grandiose claims take the form of describing the Budget as 'a Budget for jobs'. On other occasions there are wild estimates about money available for tax cuts – reductions in the standard rate of income tax and the level of tax allowances which are certain to follow. The second phase of the 'Lawson cycle' comes in January or February and takes the form of an economic crisis. [In 1985] it was the collapse of the pound which reduced the sterling exchange rate to barely more than one dollar. [In 1986] it was the collapse in oil prices which reduced the Treasury revenue by about £5 billion. Stage one is related to Stage two by the fact that the early boasting contributes to the latter collapse. In 1985 the Chancellor gave the impression that a depreciated pound would increase the fiscal adjustment from which he could finance tax cuts. This encouraged speculators to believe that there was no sterling value at which he would stand and fight. [The 1986] collapse of oil prices – although not the Chancellor's responsibility – had an unreasonable effect on the exchange rate because the neglect of manufacturing industry (in pursuit of the Chancellor's other objectives) had made the British economy peculiarly dependent on oil revenues. The emphasis on the dependence of tax cuts on sterling and oil prices did not help confidence. The third phase of the 'Cycle' is more difficult to define, for it contains confusing elements – Treasury leaks. But it is always characterised by unreasonably high interest rates which damage the prospects of industrial investment and increase the difficulties of home owners. Interest rates are held high in order to compensate for the 'Cycle's' crisis phase which the earlier boasting has intensified. But although some of the third stage characteristics are obscured by the leaks and counter leaks one eventual feature is always recognisably the same. The promises of December are not fulfilled. The Budget which promised jobs and tax cuts delivers neither. So attempts are made to divert attention from the failure by the announcements of future tax innovation. [Julius Silverman Memorial Lecture, Birmingham, 11 March 1986].

I am a great subscriber to the view that ultimately 'it is Governments that lose elections, not Oppositions that win them'. Re-establishing the Labour Party's economic policy as a credible alternative has been important. But the role played in closing the gap between Labour and Tories by the general public's perception of Government economic incompetence cannot be underestimated. Labour's boost in the polls relative to the Tories in early 1985 coincided both with Labour's decision to emphasise public investment expenditure rather than tax cuts, and with the collapse of sterling to just above parity with the dollar.

Labour's attitude to sterling has undergone a number of changes since 1983. This reflects in part the scale of the depreciation that has gone on since then and in part a reassessment of the likely inflationary impact of large scale depreciation. For a depreciation to 'work', it must involve a relative (and perhaps an absolute) fall in real wages. This point seems to be lost on those advocates of further massive devaluations. No doubt those same people would aggressively oppose those Conservatives who have advocated direct wage cutting on the grounds the latter is against the interests of the working class. Indeed the inflationary consequences of the post-1983 fall have been avoided only by the simultaneous fall in oil and other commodity prices. Great care has been taken since 1983 to emphasise that Labour would balance the competitive advantages against inflationary disadvantages of sterling depreciation. Attention to the monetary policy and inflation implications of the exchange rate is one of the reasons that entry into the European Monetary System has at least to be considered (see Chapter 6).

EXCHANGE CONTROLS

It has also been necessary for Labour to adopt a more sensible policy towards exchange control than re-introduction of pre-1979 statutory controls. The impact of simple reintroduction would almost certainly be the massive downward pressure on sterling that its advocates claim they wish to avoid (see Chapter 6). Over the year to January 1985, Labour's City and economic advisers put together a scheme based on the withdrawal of the fiscal privileges of those managed funds that did not repatriate part of their overseas investment portfolios to the UK. This scheme was examined by tax experts in the private sector and the Inland Revenue before it was finally unveiled publically. This tax-based version of exchange control was passed by Labour conference in 1985 as a replacement for statutory controls.

A few advocates of statutory controls still remain. Unfortunately they give the impression that they do not know what an exchange control is or what its effects might be. Indeed advocacy of statutory controls is probably more important as evidence of one's left-wing credentials than of one's grasp of the economic difficulties likely to be faced by an incoming Labour Government.

There are some in the Labour Party who think that a Labour Government will be automatically hit by an exchange rate crisis. Indeed they seem to regard the scale of depreciation of sterling under a Labour Government as a litmus test of its commitment to socialism. They are at the same time critical if Labour's frontbench cannot devise measures of economic autarky to prevent a run on sterling and suspicious of measures which take account of the constraints imposed by the international capitalist system:

> The idea that Britain alone can stick out against and beat the constraints of international markets seems to me to be pure fantasy. Now, we can insulate ourselves from them to a degree.

The exchange controls scheme is one of the ways of stopping a run on the pound. We can insulate ourselves from capital movements and some manufacturing goods movements by limited import controls. But the international pressures, particularly if we are in a Western European environment where other Governments are taking a different view from us, will be very substantial. And it is simply courting disaster to pretend that these people do not exist, and to pretend that they do not have power and influence. I have to strike a balance between doing what's right, and doing what's possible [*Marxism Today*, October 1985].

INDUSTRY AND THE CITY

Publicly recognising that the international capital markets exist is unlikely to make them any more sympathetic to a Government determined to cut unemployment, redistribute income and revive manufacturing. If we did not know that before, that much was clear after a long round of City and industry lectures and meetings to which I accompanied Roy Hattersley between 1984 and 1986. Although at every meeting we attended we were assured that our hosts were apolitical and did not support any political party even if they donated to one, it was difficult not to be reminded of Bernard Donaghue's remark that Labour's open supporters in the City could comfortably fit into a London taxi.

The newspapers portrayed this round of meetings as Labour's attempt to woo the City. They were in fact the result of a vast number of unsolicited invitations which were sparked off by a combination of favourable opinion polls and interest in policy innovations such as proposals for a British Investment Bank (Chapter 10), a reform of Government borrowing (Chapter 5) and an alternative to exchange control (Chapter 6).

Those visits enabled a useful exchange of views and opinions. Indeed they gave an opportunity to listen to the arguments against tough City regulation from those who subsequently shot to fame and misfortune as a result of the Guinness scandals. Frequent visits to the lions den convinced Hattersley that not all the lions wanted to eat him alive – but they did make him rather keen on lion taming. His views on City regulation are set out in Chapter 9.

When contrasted to the opinions expressed by industrialists, the City meetings also reinforced the view that there are severe problems of short-term thinking and City/industry relations – particularly with respect to the supply of long-term finance. A number of engineering employers indicated that they agreed far more with Labour's industrial policy than with the Government's lack of one. However, most indicated that they would continue to vote Conservative because they did not believe Labour would carry out its policy in practice. The purpose of the dialogue with the City and industry was never to ensure sweeping Labour gains at the next election in Surrey and the other commuter counties. But an explanation of Labour's policy may have ensured some understanding of what the Party is seeking to achieve.

> I have no doubt that things can move in my direction if I can convince those whose confidence I need that whilst I'm doing things that they may ideological disapprove of, at least my arithmetic adds up [*Marxism Today*, October 1985].

It will certainly take time for a new Labour Government to be accepted by the business community.

One way this will be helped will be through the proposed publication of a White Paper shortly after the election setting out Labour's medium-term economic plans for industry and employment. This will indicate the details of Labour's jobs programme and the expected path for key economic variables. Initially the expansion Labour proposes will require extra raw materials and extra capital equipment that will in part have to be imported from abroad. It is therefore essential to indicate how the Party sees its strategy turning round the deteriorating balance of payments Labour will inherit from the Conservatives. This has to be done in a medium-term context for the traditional short-term palliatives – deflation through cuts in public expenditure especially capital spending, and increased real interest rates – serve only to exacerbate manufacturing industry's weakness and as a result increase the long-run balance of payments constraint.

Hattersley has proposed a number of specific measures to revive manufacturing including promoting new technology (Chapter 8), getting to grips with the power of the City (Chapter 9), setting up a state industrial bank to channel funds to industry (Chapter 10), tackling the feeble mergers policy which has encouraged short-term thinking (Chapter 11) encouraging more socially responsible investment by pension funds (Chapter 12) and extending social ownership and industrial democracy (Chapter 13).

> The Labour Party stands accused and convicted of wanting to interfere with the free operation of free market forces. I plead guilty and ask for innumerable other offences – past and future – to be taken into consideration [Party Conference, Bournemouth, 3 October 1985].

Indeed, Hattersley is at the forefront of the Labour Party campaign to establish itself as the Party of Production:

> I hold the view very strongly that a socialist economic policy is about the structure of the economy and the power within it. It is not about demand management of the economy . . .

> We are not going to solve our economic problems by saying 'a bit more demand, lower interest rates, let's do what Jim Prior would do'. We are going to solve our economic problems by changing the structure of the economy. If you're telling me we have failed to do that in the past, I am agreeing with you. If you are telling me I am to blame, I am disagreeing with you [*Marxism Today*, October 1985].

CONCLUSION

Economic Priorities for a Labour Government deliberately concentrates on practical policy issues. Hattersley's philosophy and ideology are comprehensively set out in his recently published book *Choose Freedom* and it is there that some more general issues such as 'markets' are tackled. The two books complement rather than compete with one another. *Choose Freedom* is concerned with liberty and equality. This book is concerned with the first steps down the road to liberty and equality – the steps that can and will be taken in the early years of a Labour Government. It is important to emphasise its limited time horizon otherwise it will be subject to the predictable criticism that is concerned mainly with the problems of the capitalist economy Labour will inherit rather than with a description of an ideal socialist economy at some future point in time.

Too often socialists have a vague sense of a Utopia that they desire and no sense of how a capitalist economy might be transformed into a more socialist one. If the socialism some people seek is a static state of secular bliss, then socialism is unachievable. We should not be surprised that Marx did not waste many words trying to describe the People's Garden Republic of Eden.

Socialism has to be a relative concept and it has to be a dynamic concept – a set of values reflected in the way in which people try to organise change in a constantly changing society. The views set out in this book, or indeed in the longer time perspective of *Choose Freedom*, make no attempt to describe a 'New Jerusalem'. But they do represent a coherent, consistent and radical set of practical proposals for a society that will rapidly become more socialist than the one we have today. And to make a society more socialist than it was when the Party was elected to power is surely the aim of any socialist government.

There will always be a healthy debate about what constitutes 'more socialist' or indeed what speed of change is economically feasible or electorally possible. The challenge to socialist critics is to produce a more radical, more electorally attractive, more practical programme for the early years of a Labour Government. To date, no one in the past eight years of Opposition had done so.

There are, of course, some Labour economic policies which will be included in the next manifesto which are not developed in this book – but none is in direct contradiction to the policies and framework put forward here. The challenge is not to find alternatives and improvements at the margin but to find a complete alternative to the policies as a whole.

It is not sufficient to argue that there will be people of opposing political parties who will agree with some chapters. That is too easy a point to score. The Labour Party's aim is to win converts to its ideas. It must never espouse a doctrine with which no one who has supported another party can possibly agree. Just because there are also feminists in the SDP and Communist Party does not discredit feminist Labour policies any more than the espousal of demand expansion by the Tory Reform Group means that Labour should not also make use of Keynesian demand management techniques.

Another reason that some socialists will reject the position set out is that Hattersley does not use the gestures, jargon and language of some of the younger, modern left:

> My speeches are open to the criticism, and always have been,
> that they don't contain the fashionable phrases and buzzwords
> [*Marxism Today*, October 1985].

Without the rhetoric some of his proposals seem less radical than
they are.

The language with which proposals are expressed is, of course,
important. A balance has to be achieved between simply
reinforcing the views of the converted and addressing the
unconverted in language to which they can relate. Hattersley has
tended to emphasise the latter, for he believes that Labour has to
convince the electorate that it is talking everyday commonsense.
And it is to the commonsense objectives of improving services by
cutting unemployment, easing poverty by reducing inequality
and increasing wealth by stimulating industrial production, that
this book is directed.

Forty years ago, during the most successful election campaign
which the Labour Party has ever fought, Clement Attlee
defined his task as 'proving that socialism and commonsense
coincide more than our critics understand.' At first reading that
battle cry does not sound the most heroic call to arms that a
leader ever made to his army. But for those of us who believe
that the path of true glory is actually putting into practice a
programme of democratic socialism; it has an irresistible
appeal. It also has the merit of being true. There are strong
practical reasons – reasons related to overall national
prosperity, as well as reasons based on concern and compassion
– for pursuing the socialist ideal of equality. And the individual
items in any Labour programme – whether it is the creation of a
National Health Service in 1945 or the use of North Sea oil
revenues to create jobs rather than finance unemployment –
have the greatest intellectual and moral justification when they
produce in members of the unbiased general public the simple
response, 'that makes sense to me'.

There will, of course, be some people within the Party who
regard the call for practicality as a betrayal of Labour's
ideological commitment. The complaint will be based on the
offensive fallacy that socialism and commonsense are mutually
exclusive. If our beliefs have any merit, they have to be capable
of application within the real world – and the real world which

follows the next general election. The new economic path which the Party has begun to chart is by any definition *socialist*. But I can – and will – argue for its merits in terms of practical necessity [Margaret Gibb Memorial Lecture, Newcastle, 30 March 1985].

2 Putting Jobs First*

THE SCALE OF UNEMPLOYMENT

The first priority of the next Labour Government will be to put Britain back to work. Unemployment in this country is largely the result of Government policy – a policy which thrives within a jungle of economic nonsense which the Government has carefully cultivated.

In Great Britain almost four million men and women are unemployed. Over 1 300 000 of them have been unemployed for more than a year; 600 000 for more than two years. On average a redundant worker has to wait nine months before finding a new job. The cost in poverty and personal suffering needs no description. The cost to the national economy is too often overlooked. Our workers are – or should be – a national asset. Keeping so many of them idle is simply a waste of Britain's earning capacity. Every man and woman who is unemployed actually costs the Exchequer between £6000 and £7000 a year in benefits and lost tax income. The total bill for unemployment pay is now £20 billion a year – five times as much as the Government obtains in North Sea oil revenue. To repeat the facts of unemployment is to demonstrate the heartless lunacy of the politics which have created it.

The next election will – to a great extent – be fought on the rival parties' capacity to manage the economy. What each of them says about unemployment will have a major effect on the result. A party which provides an inadequate or unconvincing response to the unemployment crisis should neither win nor deserve to win.

The Conservative tactic is to duck the challenge altogether. The Chancellor offers vague platitudes about his hopes of unemployment falling.

The best that the Chancellor can offer is a modest but far from certain expansion of the service industries. Indeed, since the Conservatives came to power in 1979 our share of world invisible trade has fallen faster than our share of world manufacturing trade.

* Based on Aneurin Bevan Memorial Lecture, Redditch Town Hall, 14 October 1984; and speech to Ruskin Fellowship, House of Commons, London, 15 May 1984.

Many of the Government's claims about a 'productivity miracle' – particularly in manufacturing industry – have been based on the destruction of some of our less efficient factories. They have then claimed the destruction as a rise in productivity – fiddling the batting averages by dropping the tail enders. That is gross misuse of statistics. Resources previously employed are now unemployed. It *must* be better for the tail enders to contribute to a greater total – even if the team average is reduced.

The Government's claims concerning increased productivity are based on a fallacy. If the economy is *ever* to recover, the men and women who are not employed must go back to work and the machines which are now idle must start up again. There is no evidence that they will be more productive at the end of a decade of devastation than they were when they were in full production. We all welcome extra output from using labour and capital more efficiently. But that is very different from leaving vast natural resources unemployed and claiming a spurious victory on the basis of the results of the few left in business.

DISPELLING DOUBTS ABOUT LABOUR'S ALTERNATIVE

There was in the country in 1983 a widespread acceptance that the present Government would not reduce unemployment. However, some doubt remained about Labour's alternative. The public recognised our good intentions. But although they applauded our compassion, they doubted our capacity.

The doubts had two causes. The first was our apparent inability to offer a convincing alternative counter-inflation policy to replace the Conservative technique of price control by deflation and slump. It is said that our policy is dependent on making an agreement on incomes with the Trade Unions – an agreement which our critics claim cannot be made.

I am anxious to see an agreement between Government and unions on every aspect of economic management – including the level of wage increases which is consistent with our other economic objectives. The absence of such an agreement will not, in the circumstances we inherit, make a reduction in unemployment impossible. But to achieve an agreement on incomes – salaries, dividends and wages – would mean that we could move towards our goals at extra speed. Indeed, it would mean that we could set ourselves, and could achieve, far more ambitious goals. The Party and the Unions have agreed the following order of priorities. Resources must be devoted to the reduction of unemployment first, the low paid second and the rest of the population third.

The second cause of doubt about our economic alternative was the impression which we sometimes gave that full employment will be easily achieved. The assertion that a massive increase in effective demand would be a certain and automatic remedy is not convincing. For the task before us grows daily more formidable. We have already endured years of recession and industrial decline. It will be a great deal more difficult to get Britain back to work in 1988 than it would have been in 1983.

North Sea oil production and revenues peaked in 1986. We have missed the opportunity to use the years of peak revenues to reinvigorate the economy.

There has been a massive reduction in productive industrial capacity.

What appears to be spare capacity may in some cases no longer be suitable for use.

The increased demand which we generate may, initially, attract the products of more healthy foreign economies, producing a balance of payments constraint on our expansion.

Apprenticeships and genuine training schemes have been so reduced that, in the upturn, there will be an inhibiting shortage of skilled manpower.

The skill shortage will be intensified by the effect of long-term unemployment on workers who are forced to spend years away from their trades.

New techniques developed in economies working nearer to capacity will only be available in Britain by licence or purchase and after considerable delay.

For all these reasons, by 1988 – at the end of a full decade of high unemployment – simply reversing the Government's policies will not be enough to rectify the problem which they have caused.

To agree that generating new jobs is not easy is not the same as declaring that it is impossible. Indeed, conceding that the difficulties exist is the first step towards convincing the doubters that we know how the problem can be overcome. And we are, of course, equipped with one advantage which the Conservative

Party does not possess. We are not hampered by the ideological prejudices which prevent them from taking rational action to generate new jobs – notably an irrational opposition to borrowing and public expenditure. To cut the unemployment total by one million in two years will require us to take 1370 people off the dole every day. Such reduction has previously only been achieved in wholly exceptional conditions. The Tories will not attempt to change the economic climate in order to make conditions exceptionally favourable to job creation.

WHERE ARE THE UNEMPLOYED?

The Government has not acted against high unemployment because they have a vested interest in high unemployment. They have used it as their incomes policy. And they have welcomed it as a way of shifting power towards big business. In industrial relations compromise and conciliation have been replaced by the threat of the sack. The Government has encouraged wage cuts for many low-paid workers and imposed wage cuts in the public sector. These policies could not have been pursued without the existence of mass unemployment.

Indeed, the Government is now so committed to high unemployment that it attempts to define economic recovery in a way that excludes any reduction in unemployment. A definition of recovery that does not include putting Britain back to work is not acceptable in a civilised society – especially when we know that unemployment can be drastically reduced by the continuous application of an alternative set of policies: economic and industrial, national and regional.

As well as ensuring equal opportunities for women, the ingredients in that package must be directly related to the groups and areas where unemployment is highest.

There are vast regional disparities – unemployment in the North is almost twice as great as in the South East. In the West Midlands it is half as great again as it is within the East Midlands.

Differences *within* regions are greater than differences *between* them. The inner cities and towns once dependent upon now obsolescent industries suffer from intensified unemployment.

The ethnic minorities are particularly badly affected – partly because of overt or unconscious discrimination, partly because they live and work in areas where the depression has hit the hardest.

Young workers are the worst affected – 35 per cent of the unemployment total comes from the 16 to 25 age group. But it is the over 55s who face the greatest risk of long-term unemployment.

Manufacturing industry has been hit harder than services – of the jobs lost since 1979, almost two million have been in manufacturing.

THE GOVERNMENT VIEW

The Government both shrugs off responsibility for this multiple crisis and claims that the provision of a remedy is beyond its power. The Chancellor insists that 'the Government can only provide the right framework within which change will take place more smoothly'. In 1979 they promised full employment – lower prices 'without a significant loss of output'. Then they promised that as inflation fell unemployment would fall too. Now they will not predict significant real falls in unemployment from its present level in the foreseeable future. They pretend that it does not matter.

The Chancellor told a House of Commons select Committee that he does 'not believe in all this business about fiscal expansion'. The truth is that he does not believe in all this business about reducing unemployment. Contemporary right-wing philosophy rejects the idea that the Government either can or should act to reduce unemployment. That is one of the major ideological differences that divide the Conservative and Labour Parties. We believe it to be the Government's moral duty to generate new jobs. And we have no doubt that it is possible. That judgement differs from the Chancellor's in that it is based on the reality of evidence not the fantasy of dogma.

The truth is that two million jobs have been lost in manufacturing in the last eight years in large part because of the Government's exchange rate policy (which priced our goods out of foreign markets in the early 1980s), and its tight money policy which drove so many companies to contraction and bankruptcy. Yet the Government persists in its pretence that unemployment has risen for reasons wholly outside its control. Two Tory excuses have achieved wholly unjustified acceptance. The first is that most unemployment has been the result of world recession not domestic policy. The second is the allegation that the level of welfare benefits is so generous that it acts as a disincentive to work. Let us dispose of both fallacies.

In 1979 when the Tories came to power the level of unemployment in the UK was about the same as the average for the EEC. It is now much higher than the EEC average. In the United Kingdom the rate of job loss between 1979 and 1984 exceeded that in virtually every other OECD country. Britain entered recession before most other countries. Indeed, far from international factors causing Britain's mass unemployment, the UK led the rest of the world into recession, and President Reagan's adoption of policies similar to Mrs Thatcher's in the early 1980s exacerbated the drift towards slump. Obviously Britain was affected by the growing popularity of monetarism in other countries. But North Sea oil should have sheltered us from the worst ravages of the recession as it sheltered Norway.

The argument that blames relatively high unemployment benefits for rising unemployment can be easily dismissed. The abolition of earnings related benefits, the taxation of unemployment and supplementary benefits and real cuts in benefit levels has meant that lower and lower real earnings offer a higher standard of living than unemployment pay. If the theory that rising unemployment pay caused rising unemployment were accurate the relative fall in benefit levels would have caused unemployment to fall. That has not happened. Unemployment has continued to rise dramatically. In the UK there are 215 000 job vacancies notified to the Department of Employment and four million men and women seeking work. Even if some of the unemployed are deterred from seeking work by the rate of benefit, many others would be willing to take their places. The net effect of benefit levels is negligible. Life on the dole is far from comfortable and it would be extraordinary if – with an average expected duration of nine months' unemployment – a significant number of unemployed workers deliberately refused jobs.

THE ALTERNATIVE

But the problem which the nation faces requires us to do more than allocate blame. We must begin by reversing some of the policies which – all objective observers agree – have caused unemployment to rise. Reversing those policies is not, in itself, enough. But an essential beginning is an increase in demand that is targeted on domestic production and the maintenance of a stable exchange rate which does not penalise exporters and assist importers. There will, of course, need to be an increase in the budget deficit. Even the Chancellor of the Exchequer admits that an increase in the PSBR or budget deficit does not lead to an automatic escalation of interest rates. In recent years we have had a relatively small budget deficit and record real interest rates. So we ought to be spared any more nonsense about an increase in public spending financed by borrowing causing such desperate damage to the prospect for private investment that the cure is worse than the disease.

Even if a rise in the budget deficit leads to some increase in interest rates there is no evidence that private investment will be 'crowded out'. Indeed, the reverse is likely to be true. In virtually every other industrialised country in the early and mid 1980s the budget deficit was higher than it was in Britain – yet unemployment was lower than in the United Kingdom. Both the IMF and the OECD have estimated that we actually ran a structural budget surplus at that time. That is to say that if, at the rates of spending and taxation then current, we approached full employment, Government income would have exceeded expenditure.

The expansion of expenditure financed by borrowing must be carefully channelled towards those areas which most readily generate employment. And it must be augmented by a whole series of structural changes in the economy. We do not argue with the Chancellor's contention that changes are needed on the supply side. His error lies both with the type of supply-side policies which he favours and in his assumption that such changes will, in themselves, be enough to generate activity. He seems to think of supply-side changes simply in terms of simplifying the tax system: privatising services of profitable publicly owned industry and reducing the power of Trade Unions. He ignores the inhibiting effects of monopolies, mergers and the restraint of competition, the need for improvement in the infrastructure, the often inadequate ways in which we finance new industrial investment, the need for improved training and increased

expenditure on research and development and strategic use of
public funds to assist high technology companies.

The increases we propose in the budget deficit will best fulfil our
aims if they are concentrated on public spending rather than tax
reduction. According to the Treasury a tax cut of £1½ billion
(1 per cent off the standard rate of income tax) reduced
unemployment by only about 20 000 jobs after two years. The
same amount directed into public spending reduces
unemployment to 120 000. It is, of course, in the construction
industry that the opportunities are the most obvious. But
throughout the public service there are social needs that can be
met by policies which breathe life into the economy. That, of
course, implies the need to expand current as well as capital
spending. Building a new hospital provides no benefit unless
nurses and doctors are employed to staff it. The first opportunity
for direct job creation is in the public sector.

Unlike the Government we must avoid the mistake of writing
off manufacturing industry. But we must accept the difficulty of
recreating all of the jobs which have been lost in manufacturing
during the last eight years. There is scope for expansion in the
private services. But Department of Employment research
suggests that even a 3 per cent annual growth rate would only
raise private sector service employment by 160 000 a year.

So we cannot rely on the private service sector to generate jobs
on the necessary scale. That is why public spending is so vital.
Public spending on capital projects has a complementary effect on
public and private jobs – increased school building increases jobs
for construction workers, the suppliers of building components
and nursery school teachers. Public spending on social services
improves the health and comfort of our population and generates
jobs.

So in contrast to the Government we support the initiatives
taken by the CBI and TUC in drawing up lists of necessary capital
projects in the public sector. But the generalised reflation which
will result from such a programme will not be enough in itself to
counteract the effects of structural unemployment – the decline
and collapse of old industries which has been accelerated by
Government policy. We are well aware of the constraints of
reflation. There can be no dash for growth. But a successful
general expansion is the necessary backdrop to those structural
and institutional steps which we will take to generate jobs.

In fact, the Government cannot remain passive and hope that jobs will eventually be generated. Any Government should – and a Labour Government will – actively promote employment creating projects. This Administration talks only about removing constraints. What we need is positive action. It is, for instance, plainly unfair that the chances of being re-employed in the North of England are far less than in the South East. But with a restrictive monetary policy all that regional initiatives can achieve is diversion from one hard pressed area to another. A more expansionist economic policy would permit regional and urban intervention to generate extra jobs instead of simply shifting jobs around.

The same principle applies to industrial training. We cannot run successful programmes if most of the workers who complete them graduate to the dole queues. Nor is there any virtue in giving tax concessions to small companies, if, at the same time, the continual fiscal squeeze produces a record number of insolvencies.

To generate output and jobs the control of public spending has to be liberated from the abstraction of the Medium Term Financial Strategy [see Chapter 3]. It is wholly absurd that the centrepiece of our economic strategy should be the Public Sector Borrowing Requirement – a grossly inaccurate assessment of the residual difference between the huge estimates of revenue and expenditure. It is not a calculation but a guess as the invariable discrepancies between forecast and outturn show. But it has become the totem around which the City of London and the Treasury dances [see Chapter 5]. Liberated from such superstition the Labour Party has developed detailed policies which:

1. Have removed the constraints of the Medium Term Financial Strategy by demonstrating its intellectual shortcomings and by putting in its place a sensible fiscal and monetary policy.
2. Replaced Conservative Micawberism with a programme of public expenditure in the trading sector which is directed specifically to employment generation through:
- infrastructure spending on roads, railways and housing to reverse the massive deterioration in our social capital which has taken place since 1979
- an expansion of training to reverse the savage cut in the apprentice intake that the recession has caused

- more public funds directed to research and development
3. Further expenditure in the public non-trading sector which simultaneously improves welfare and creates jobs – for example, an expansion of pre-school education and care for the elderly.

We have defined the structural changes in our financial institutions which are required to achieve this programme [Ch. 10]. And we have avoided the old Department of Industry approach which attempted to 'pick winners' but too often ended with support for losers. And we have recognised that a vigorous competition policy will improve the overall performance of the economy [Ch. 11].

The Conservatives have thought it necessary to its policy to change the relationship between Government and organised labour. It will be equally necessary, for the success of our policy, to change the relationship between the Government and the City of London [Ch. 9].

The men and women who create our wealth and contribute to our welfare must be given a greater opportunity to participate in the decisions which affect their working lives. Their expertise and increased enthusiasm will become invaluable assets [Ch. 13].

Our principal policy objective is putting Britain back to work. It is an objective which we can and will achieve.

3 The Medium-term Financial Strategy*

IMPACT OF THE MTFS

For years the Government has never tired of telling us that its economic policy is built around and dependent upon the Medium Term Financial Strategy. Despite the air of mystery which surrounds that strategy, its basic ideas are simple. Indeed, they are too simple. The MTFS is an intellectually unsophisticated policy. It has been applied with a lack of subtlety but with an excess of evangelical zeal. The method of its application – almost as much as the central error in its concept – has produced calamitous results for the United Kingdom economy. The Medium Term Financial Strategy produced a 2 000 000 increase in the unemployment total, a slump in investment, a collapse of manufacturing, and annual tax bill which has grown by £29 500 million, the highest real interest rates in our history, record numbers of company liquidations, an increase in poverty, a widening gap between the rich and the poor and massive cuts in public services – all this despite the uncovenanted bonus of North Sea oil revenues.

Those indisputable features of the new British economy have been justified by the Government with the slogan that there is no alternative – that only hard decisions, resolute action, rigid commitment to established financial targets and the acceptance of what was crudely called good housekeeping standards could produce eventual economic recovery. Initially there was a substantial political bonus to be gained from inflexibility. But inflexibility is not an end in itself. The rigidity has to produce the desired effect. At first we were told that the MTFS could bring down inflation without increasing unemployment and undermining the real economy. Then the prediction was adjusted to the assurance that the loss of jobs and output would be only temporary. Now there are no predictions or promises of success. Nor can there be. For the MTFS is inherently incapable of

* Based on Oxford University Business School Lecture, 13 September 1984.

37

providing a framework within which the problems of the real economy are solved.

From its inception the Medium Term Financial Strategy was never as succesful as its supporters claimed. It was incompetently applied. Perhaps for that we ought to give thanks. For if the targets which the Government set had been hit the effects on the real economy would have been still more disastrous. The principal criticism of the MTFS is not the lack of competence with which it was applied – obvious though that shortcoming is. The real condemnation is that however the MTFS was applied it would have resulted in a deep depression and massive increases in unemployment. Both these results are inherent within the strategy. The strategy can be easily described. It embraces monetarism and a particular version of supply-side economics. To the Government reform of the supply-side means no more than a limitation on Trade Union power, arcane adjustments to the tax structure and the abandonment of Government intervention in the economy. Fiscal policy is dismissed as an instrument of economic management and replaced by monetary control. Inherent in the doctrine is faith in the operation of markets. For in the MTFS the Government holds the ring. It plays little or no part in the actual contest. The theory behind the MTFS has centred on two propositions:

(a) There is a systematic relationship between the money supply and the rate of inflation which ensures that control of the money supply will eventually produce stable prices.
(b) That public sector borrowing has a direct and automatic effect on interest rates and, thus, increases in public borrowing reduce private investment.

The argument concerning this 'financial crowding out' is complicated by the Government's application of rigid monetary targets. It may be that, given a firm target for monetary growth, the effect which the Government fears applies over a run of years. But that is an argument for making monetary targets meet the demands of the real economy, not for requiring the real economy to accept the penalties of fixed monetary targets. The certainty – in the minds of the medium term financial strategists – is that a rigid macro-financial framework will hold down inflation. Their related hope is that the public insistence that such targets are to be set and achieved will reduce inflationary expectations. If wage negotiators respond to the promise of reduced prices, the inflationary path will fall even more steeply. If they do not, as long as the monetary targets are observed, the result will be increasing unemployment levels.

REASONS FOR FAILURE

Before we expose the inherent conceptual inadequacies of the MTFS, it is necessary to examine some of its specific failures – the reasons which prevented the theory from even working within the Government's own terms:

(a) The belief that movements in the money supply produce an automatic movement in prices depends upon the velocity of circulation of money remaining relatively stable. The evidence of the last decade demonstrates that the idea of such stability is a fiction. What is more, the Government added to instability by its policy of banking deregulation. And recent innovations in the financial sector intensified the process. The result was that £M3 was substantially off target, even when other indicators suggested that the monetary stance was substantially too tight.

(b) Any hope of an immediate effect on inflationary expectation was dashed by the increase in Value Added Tax which the Chancellor included in his first Budget of 1979. The political purpose of that decision was a shift from direct to indirect taxation. Its financial intention was to ensure no increase in the PSBR. The result was an increase in prices. Increasing prices in order to cut inflation was a spectacular victory for the theoretical over the real economy.

(c) By its nature, the policy created economic conditions which increased rather than reduced the PSBR. The reduction in activity cut income tax and corporation tax revenues. The increase in unemployment pushed up welfare expenditure.

(d) The Government's decision to engineer an increase in interest rates, which (although against the general tenets of its policy) was thought necessary in the short term to hold down the rate of growth in the money supply had results quite the opposite of what the Government expected. £M3 included interest bearing deposits and therefore that ingredient increased when interest rates went up. Firms faced with higher servicing costs for their capital increased their borrowing to meet their new obligations.

(e) The combined effect of a Government induced slump, increasing oil production and a monetary policy tight to the point of strangulation produced a severely over valued pound. The high exchange rate produced, in turn, a disastrous effect on the international competitiveness of British industry. The result was the first British trade deficit in manufactured goods since the Industrial Revolution.

It may also be that the Government's strength of purpose was sapped by the effect of even the inadequately executed MTFS on the real economy. Certainly in 1982 the Government's resolution faltered. Credit controls were relaxed. Public expenditure constraints were slightly eased. A mini-boom resulted. The charitable explanation concerns the rising tide of unemployment, the cynical relates to the general election. Whatever the reason the single-mindedness temporarily evaporated.

These failures are more than examples of Government operational incompetence. That they certainly demonstrate. But they reveal something more fundamental. Such errors were unavoidable in a policy which chose to place too much of its faith in the result of meeting two arbitrary targets, and required all other economic objectives to become subservient to the achievement of those target figures. It was a policy which suffered from a major confusion between ends and means.

Between them these results of the MTFS produced for Britain a slump which hit our economy earlier than the world recession hit the rest of Europe and resulted, when the world recession came, in our slump biting deeper and lasting longer than that in any of our competitor's economies. Of course the massive deflation of the economy also had some effect on inflation. But the strategy was not supposed to work that way. Its originators did not consciously decide to destroy manufacturing industry by pricing it out of export markets through an over valued pound. Nor did they plan to cripple the construction industry by ending its public sector contracts. They no doubt shared my view that any fool can cut inflation by collapsing the economy. They believed that the MTFS would achieve the lower inflation rate by a quite different process from that which brought it about.

It is possible that the Government did anticipate *some* immediate damage to the real economy but chose to disregard it. The London Business School, from whence the wisdom of the MTFS flowed, always argued that the transmission mechanism from tight money to inflationary expectations and on into prices was a high exchange rate. But the LBS believed that a higher exchange rate would feed through into prices and wages very quickly and that little output would be lost. The Government hoped that the consequent reduction in the import costs of both manufactured goods and raw materials would lower some costs and squeeze profit margins by the increase it provided in foreign competition. If British goods became uncompetitive – especially as the result of high wage costs – workers would lose their jobs as the penalty for the failure to adjust their inflationary expectations.

The *willingness* to sacrifice the real economy was always a feature of the MTFS. But such was the Government's faith in the theory that the damage was expected to be both slight and temporary. It has turned out to be deep and prolonged. In part its length and severity is the result of the Government's initial inability to consider the possibility that the MTFS could be conceptually wrong. The Government was prepared to make a slight alteration in the ingredients of its prescription. But it never even considered the possibility that the medicine was fundamentally damaging. A new prescription was never considered – so:

(a) When £M3 severely overshot its targets – for the reasons which we have already observed are inherent in the strategy – the Government, guided by its exclusive concern for the money supply, ignored all the other indicators which suggested that a relaxation was necessary.

(b) Equally when the PSBR overshot its targets – for reasons equally concerned with the policy itself – the Government embarked on a new round of public expenditure cuts.

The inevitable result was a further deterioration in the patient's condition.

CHANGES IN THE MTFS

The money supply target at which the Government hs aimed over the last five years has, of course, been changed. No doubt the new definitions of money supply have owed something to the political compulsion to find a target which can be hit. And no doubt the changes in the monetary aggregates to be targeted were mainly the product of the Government's genuine wish to find an instrument by which it could first measure and then control monetary growth. It is inconceivable that it will succeed, particularly with the financial system changing so rapidly. Each measurement of the money supply is continually changing in character so that the idea of its growth also determining the conduct of the whole economy is particularly implausible.

Yet the Government has abandoned any attempt to guide the course of the real economy. Indeed, it is argued from time to time that such guidance is either impossible or undesirable. It is the almost mystical reliance on these two factors – money supply and PSBR – and these two factors alone, which sets the MTFS apart from any government economic strategy which has been employed since the war. I do not argue for a moment that the next Labour Government will have no concern for the money supply and public borrowing. The last Labour Government was – as our opponents never cease to tell us – concerned about both aggregates. But this Government apparently believes (and certainly behaves as if it believes) that money supply and PSBR are all that matter. As a result essential Government action is neglected. And the two objectives which make up their policy are pursued with such fervour that they are intensified when their effects are clearly damaging to the economy. Of course, the calamitous consequences are compounded by the simple fact that the theory which promotes them to such importance is wrong. It is wrong because it places far too much faith in both the relationship between the money supply and inflation and the Government's ability to control the money supply.

The Government concentrated not on the results it needed – lower inflation and greater growth – but on the technique by which it hoped to bring it about. The method became an objective in itself. Instead of attacking the disease, the Government assaulted the symptoms.

In the early days of the policy the Government argued for free wage bargaining on the principle that, since inflation was a purely monetary phenomenon, the tight control of money would provide an automatic compensating mechanism. If wage negotiators were slow to learn the lesson, their unreasonable demands would simply increase unemployment. Then, when inflationary expectations were adjusted, wage demands would be moderated and industrial growth would begin. Of course, it has not happened like that. Indeed, the Government has now adjusted its position. It still blames unemployment on wages. But the automatic adjustment is no longer adequate to avoid inflation. So, there is what amounts to a wages policy in the public sector and massive exhortation to moderation in the private. The truth is that workers and those who negotiate on their behalf have become inoculated against the fear of unemployment. The total is now well above the once inconceivable figure of 3 million. Workers do not believe that wage increases caused the total to rise to that level. Nor do they believe that wage moderation will cause the total to fall by holding down inflation. The result was an old-fashioned slump – inflation reduced by the same processes that held down prices in the 1920s and early 1930s.

An examination of the vicissitudes of sterling demonstrated further intellectual and practical flaws in the MTFS. The exchange rate, the Tories argued, had to be determined by the markets, as a free float was essential to a control of the money supply. It is not – according to their theories – possible to have both tight monetary targets and exchange rate targets. The free float has been an obvious and admitted disaster. In 1980–1 the value of sterling was allowed to rise to absurdly high levels as the result of the sudden inflow of oil revenues. The effect on jobs and exports was deeply damaging. Then in 1984 the exchange rate began to deteriorate – partly because of the strength of the dollar, partly because of the Government's public insistence that it had no exchange rate policy. The Government's reaction to the January crisis exposed the absurdity of the whole interlocking system of related (but unrealistic) theories.

It was the recantation – of the notion that the exchange rate is best determined by market forces which marked the public rejection of the *laissez-faire* philosophy. The January 1985 sterling crisis ended with the official abandonment of two items of previous faith. The Government intervened in the market and bought sterling in the hope of protecting its value. The Government first encouraged an increase in interest rates and then reinstituted Minimum Lending Rates in order that it could act directly to set the highest real interest rate in our history. A 14

per cent interest rate was, of course, deeply damaging to the
prospect of industrial investment and the direct cause of the sharp
increase in mortgage rates. The vacillation and panic which
accompanied the crisis probably did as much to damage the
Government's reputation as the high rate itself. But the deep
underlying damage came from the tacit admission that when the
crisis came, the old free market shibboleths had to be abandoned.
Laissez-faire got Britain into the mess. For speculators were
encouraged to believe that there was no exchange rate for which
the Chancellor would stand and fight. Government intervention
was the technique chosen to limit the damage. The increase in
interest rates to 14 per cent was, of course, another proof that the
public borrowing theory on which the Government has based its
hope of economic progress was also fundamentally flawed.

The Mansion House address of 1985 gave an indication of the
new monetary policy:

(a) The idea that there is no systematic relationship between
various definitions of the money supply and nominal GDP is
now admitted. The Government has declared that its
inability to hit their sterling M3 no longer matters. The basic
tenet of monetarism – in defence of which so many firms have
been driven to bankruptcy, so many social services cut, so
many jobs lost – has been abandoned.

(b) The crude Medium Term Financial Strategy, based on a
blinkered attempt to maintain rigid adherence to a small
number of simple pre-announced intermediate targets is
rejected. Policy discretion – responding to a number of
monetary indicators – is now in vogue. The Medium Term
Financial Strategy now means whatever the Government
wants it to mean.

(c) It has, in effect, been admitted that the free float policy for
sterling was a disaster. The G5 agreement of 1985 signalled a
reversal of the Government's previous opposition to
international financial co-operation. There is now – in effect –
an exchange rate target band. Sterling is kept high by the
Government's policy of holding up short term interest rates.

The significance of the Mansion House revelations was not that
they marked a change in Government policy. It simply admitted
the changes which had gone on since the January 1985 sterling
crisis.

APPRAISAL OF THE MTFS

All that has been new about that MTFS insofar as it can be regarded as a strategy at all is the mumbo-jumbo and the evangelical fervour with which it has been applied. The result – unemployment, stagnant output and low investment – could have been achieved in a number of different ways. The Government's originality is limited to its concentration on means rather than ends, techniques instead of results. Money supply ought to be consistent with an acceptable level of inflation and unemployment. And the PSBR should produce the same result. Because of the Government's bizarre decision to stand the relationship between objectives and methods on its head, we ended up with lower levels of employment, investment, output and exports as the Government sought to make them consistent with its money supply and PSBR targets.

The justification for elevating systems above solutions was the conviction and the promise that if we had hit the mystic numbers all the other aspects of the economy would have automatically come right. They have not come right and will not come right. Now the Government does not even make any prediction about when substantial real reductions in unemployment will come. We are assured that they are certain, that one day all the poverty and suffering will seem worthwhile. But no-one tells us when that day will be. The fruits of the MTFS – assuming that they are not simply the achievement of arbitrarily chosen levels of money supply and public spending – disappear before us as we advance towards them. Not even inflation is as low as the Government promised and intended.

We need to be clear what, in the real world of the British economy, has happened over recent years. Unemployment has acted as a sort of incomes policy. An overvalued pound reduced exports and reduced import prices. Commodity prices collapsed. That fall in inflation experienced by the United Kingdom has been no better than that in the OECD as a whole, whilst the rise in unemployment has been worse. What has been achieved by and during the MTFS has been won at a terrible price in terms of the real economy – its employment level, its manufacturing output, its exports and its investment.

The great achievement of the present Government – inspired by the Prime Minister herself – has been the way in which it has succeeded in persuading so many people that policies which have either failed or are certain to fail are either succeeding or certain to succeed in the future. It is a bonus gained from what the Prime Minister calls conviction politics – views held with such unthinking certainty that the possibility of their being wrong is not even contemplated.

4 Fiscal Policy – Public Expenditure and Taxation*

NO DASH FOR GROWTH

The days of the Keynesian 'dash for growth' (based on a sudden pre-Election spurt in consumption spending only to be followed by a post-Election balance of payments crisis) are over – at least for the Labour Party. We must all learn from the experience of the French Socialist Government, where an overambitious expansion had to be reversed. The next Labour Government is not going to begin with the bang of overambitious expansion and end with the whimper of deflation and contraction. We are inclined to say now, that 'stop–go' is better than continuous stop. But this 'stop–go' cycle played havoc with both industry and the local authorities. It made it difficult for them to set longer-term investment plans with any degree of certainty. The result was that the 'stop–go' cycle only served to disguise, yet reinforce industry's long-term relative decline.

This has led some – many on the right but also a significant number of socialists – to abandon Keynesian demand policies for supply-side policy. That is wrong. Effective supply-side policy is inevitably linked to sensible demand policies and vice-versa. Structural change and industrial policy are easier against the background of a steady and high level of demand, whilst any given Government boost to demand will result in a higher level of UK output if the Government takes care to plan and direct at least some of that demand right through to the micro–economic level.

On this basis the next Labour Government will set out a medium-term employment and industrial strategy in consultation with representatives of both sides of industry. The primary belief that will underwrite it is that it is better to set demand at a slower

* Based on speech to Ilford Constituency Labour Party, 25 September 1985; speech to Institutional Investors Conference, New York, 11 September 1986; speech to British Institute of Management, London, 16 September 1986; speech to International Equity Dealers Conference, London, 15 January 1987.

47

pace over a number of years (provided that that level of demand can be consistently maintained) rather than indulge in a dash for growth. But even this relatively modest level of demand cannot be left to be allocated entirely by the unfettered free market. Given the appallingly weak state of the non-oil economy, much of that extra demand would simply spill abroad or be dissipated in higher prices. That is why crude Keynesianism – a doctrine never talked of outside the SDP – must be rejected in favour of planned Keynesianism.

TAX CUTS VERSUS PUBLIC EXPENDITURE

In stimulating demand there will be a bias in favour of public expenditure rather than personal tax cuts. Public expenditure can more easily be directed to the stimulation of domestic investment and employment than personal tax cuts which favour consumption – often of foreign goods.

At present, the Government is promoting unsustainable policies which will do the economy long-term harm, in the hope that they can win short-term popularity for the Conservative Party. The damage will be increased by the tax cuts which will certainly be part of the pre-election budget.

Tory ideology requires tax cuts for the rich and it opposes increases in public expenditure – in principle. It was because of that doctrinaire approach to the economy (as much as belief in the supply side of lower taxes) and the fear of public reaction against the Government's willingness to see a continual increase in the level of unemployment which prompted the Prime Minister to begin the pretence that tax cuts are the best way of increasing demand and, through increasing demand, encouraging the creation of new jobs. The deception was stated in the House of Commons on 13 December 1984.

On that day, in an answer to a question from me, the Prime Minister was explicit that pound for pound tax cuts create more jobs than are generated by public investment expenditure and that the increase in consumption financed by tax cuts results in a smaller addition to imports than the equivalent sums used for public sector investment:

Increasing infrastructure is not a cost-effective way in which to increase the number of jobs. The cost per job through increasing infrastructure can vary from £35 000 to £55 000. It is an expensive method, which tends to lead to a lot of hire of plant but not much hire of men. Reduction of tax can lead to extra jobs, as it leads to extra demand. The Right Hon. Gentleman's thesis that investment always leads to purchases from home sources while reduction of tax leads to purchases abroad is not correct. In an age of specialisation much of the investment in equipment and machinery goes abroad [*Hansard*, Col. 1204, 13 December 1984].

Both of these contentions are untrue. It is not for me to say if the Prime Minister's error was the result of ignorance or malice. What is clear is that Mrs Thatcher suffers from a basic confusion about her own policy. For her answer implies that an increase in demand is necessary – a view which she had previously strenuously rejected. But if the Prime Minister has really become converted to the need for an economic stimulus, one problem remains. She has chosen the wrong way to do it. According to the *Sunday Times* the Government possesses a paper which demonstrates the superiority of tax cuts:

The paper also disputes claims that more jobs would be created by investing in capital projects and public works: it states that 30% of public investment is spent on imports, compared with only 20% seeping into imports when tax thresholds are raised [*Sunday Times*, 16 December 1984].

The Chancellor has endorsed the same point. It is now official Government policy that public spending attracts more imports than does a tax reduction of the same size and that jobs are more effectively created by tax cuts than by public investment. At least it is the Prime Minister's official policy and the Chancellor's official policy. It is not the policy in which the Treasury believes. For the Treasury's examination of the problem points in the opposite direction. The Treasury's own model confirms that new jobs are far more effectively and efficiently created by public investment.

The input/output tables, published by the Department of Industry demonstrate that *public* investment attracts far less imports than does private consumption. It seems that these are the tables on which the Government bases its phoney figures. For the crude totals in their summary tables coincide with the figures which have been hawked around financial journalists. The input/output tables confirm that the import content of consumption is 20 per cent whilst the import content of investment is 30 per cent. But the summary from which the Government source quoted does not distinguish between public and private investment or between investment in construction plant and industrial machinery. Detailed figures in the table show that the construction industry attracts only 15 per cent import content. On the other hand, electrical consumer goods and man-made fibres – into which a large part of the budget-released consumer expenditure would flow – rate 41.7 per cent and 38.7 per cent import content respectively. In short, tax cuts are far more likely to stimulate jobs abroad, at the expense of British industry, than are increases in local and national Government capital programmes.

These are facts available to the Government in general and to the Chancellor in particular. The Chancellor's response to the evidence is to take cover behind the last refuge of Ministers who are confronted by the facts – cheap chauvinism. He argues that:

> To suppose that if less were taken in tax and that British people had more money in their pockets it would all be spent on textiles from Hong Kong and videos from Japan shows remarkably little faith in British industry.

Such bluster shows remarkably little faith in the evidence presented to him by his own Treasury. Much (of course, not all) of the new purchasing power would be spent on foreign goods – not least because the collapse of industry brought on by this Government has resulted in fewer and fewer British goods being available. The Chancellor is presiding over a balance of payments which, without the temporary oil revenues, would amount to national bankruptcy. An increase in consumption fuelled by tax cuts *will* suck in more imports. At least the Prime Minister has the wit to concede the danger and falsify the evidence to discount it.

TAX CUTS, THE ELECTION AND THE BALANCE OF PAYMENTS

Against the background of balance of payments difficulties and an unsustainable growth of imports there can be no justification for tax cuts in the 1987 budget. Tax cuts are the wrong prescription for the British economy. They are neither economically nor socially the right choice for this country. The Government hopes that a cut in the standard rate will both win votes and obscure the underlying danger of an impending crisis. I believe that it will do neither. Indeed, it will bring the crisis nearer. What is more, a tax cut made in March 1987 will inevitably lead to compensating action immediately the election is over. That necessity would face whatever Government was in post. Even were the Tories to win, they would reimpose higher taxes and make public expenditure cuts so deep that even the Conservative Party would be reluctant to support them. The Labour Party voted against cuts in the standard rate in 1987 and will reverse them when we are elected. We will return to approximately the present level of taxation.

There are risks in telling the electorate that the proposed tax cuts are wrong and that we will reverse them. The forecast that the Tory Party, if returned to power, would be forced to compensate for those reductions by reversing them and by massive public expenditure cuts, will be denied by the Government. The insistence that the continuation and encouragement of the consumer boom will lead to certain crisis will be rejected by the Chancellor and by those newspapers who see themselves as vehicles of Conservative policy and propaganda. But the sceptics should consider the record.

Before the General Election of 1979, the Labour Party said that if the Conservative Party came to power it would make a massive increase in VAT. The Conservative Party denied that they had any such intention. Indeed the *Daily Mail* published the accusation on its front page as one of 'Labour's Lies'. Immediately after its election the Conservative Government doubled VAT to 15 per cent. On the evidence the Conservative Party does not tell the truth about taxation before general elections. I quote from the Chancellor who doubled VAT: 'We have absolutely no intention of doubling VAT'.

If the dangers of a balance of trade crisis are deepened by tax cuts, whichever Government is elected next polling day will reverse these tax cuts. The difference is between the Labour Party, which is honest about it, and the Conservative Party, which is not.

PLANNING PUBLIC EXPENDITURE

In planning for increased public expenditure care will be taken by a Labour Government to direct it to:

(a) The purchase of UK goods and capital.
(b) The stimulation of less import intensive sectors such as construction.
(c) The encouragement of job intensive sectors in the public services and construction.

All of these measures enable us to get a bigger level of UK employment and output for a given stimulus of demand. Once we start to plan the demand stimulus we can sustain it further with other complementary measures which avoid the progress of expansion being held back by bottlenecks in the supply of trained manpower. The British National Investment Bank will ensure that finance is available on terms that promote UK investment. Training policy will be directed to supplying the skills which industry requires. We know that our programme of house building and replacement of decrepit hospitals and schools require extra bricklayers. It is common sense to train additional bricklayers. Similarly we have told the local authorities to prepare programmes of house building and other capital projects to implement immediately following the election. The certainty of demand for building materials will also enable UK suppliers to gear up in anticipation of guaranteed demand.

There is an argument which suggests that demand is currently sufficient and that any stimulus will simply result in domestic bottlenecks and extra imports. That may be the case if extra demand is indiscriminate. That is why the modified or planned Keynesianism I propose has two components. Some demand will be targeted precisely, whilst the rest – for example the second round effects of public expenditure as extra employees spend their wages – will be left to market forces.

It is worth repeating that we can only proceed as quickly as the inflation constraints allow. If we have not constructed a mechanism which allows us to expand at maximum speed with minimum inflation, then the speed of our reflation will have to be reduced. It does not, of course, mean that the expansion programme would have to be abandoned, but it will be slowed down. Our task is to so organise the economy that maximum acceleration is possible.

TORY SPENDING POLICIES AND INDUSTRY'S NEEDS

It would be difficult to design a public expenditure policy more out of phase with industry's needs than that of the present Government. The major areas of growth have been:

(a) Welfare payments and unemployment benefits – a direct result of the problems of industry, many of which originate from government economic policy.
(b) Interest payments – a burden on government that is a parallel burden on industry.
(c) Military expenditure – much of it due to go on imported weapons systems. It also accounts for a disproportionate amount of UK research and development expenditure, even though there are few spin-offs for non-military manufacturing industry.

The areas that have been cut almost invariably damaged industry. Major areas for cuts have been:

(a) Public capital expenditure and maintenance – resulting in less work for UK construction companies and suppliers and (as the CBI has complained) less efficient road and rail communications.
(b) Local authorities – both Labour and Conservative councils have been forced to raise rates on businesses because of cuts in the Central Government Rate Support Grant from over 60 per cent to less than 50 per cent.
(c) Education – education is investment in the future productivity of the labour force. Yet it has been heavily cut, often in those areas with the most potential spin-offs for industry. For example, the technological universities and polytechnics have been savaged, as has basic research. The cuts in funds for overseas students have resulted in retaliation against British manufacturing exports.
(d) Export promotion – the Export Credit Guarantee Department will be cut back severely over the next three years. This was announced shortly after the UK lost the Bosphorous Bridge Contract to the Japanese because of the inadequacy of our export support, and comes after the House of Lords Report on Overseas Trade recently recommended an increase in support.

(e) Research and Development and support for high technology – Research Councils such as the Medical Research Council, the Alvey programme and the micro-electronic support scheme have all been cut, even though support for science and technology is wholly inadequate compared with that of our competitors.
(f) Regional and urban aid – again basic aid for industry has been cut.

The inadequacy of Government policy is not confined to the domestic sphere. It continues to resist calls for an internationally co-ordinated policy of expansion to stimulate World Trade and growth and ease the problems of the US deficits and the Third World debt.

PUBLIC PURCHASING POLICY – THE MARKS AND SPENCER TECHNIQUE

It is not just the areas in which public money is spent that are important in setting out a pro-industry macro-economic policy. The way money is spent is also vital. In total £35 billion per annum – 25 per cent of all public expenditure – is spent on goods and services. It is my view that public expenditure should, wherever possible, be spent on UK products in preference to products produced overseas. Where British products of a sufficiently high standard do not exist, then the Government should approach suppliers with the offer of secure contracts in return for an improvement in supply. Like our proposals for a public sector balance sheet [see Chapter 5], the negotiated supply is another idea which we are glad to borrow from industry. It is sometimes called the 'Marks and Spencer' technique. Marks and Spencer use their huge purchasing power – over 90 per cent of which is spent in the UK – to ensure an adequate supply of the goods it wants at the right price and quality from its competing suppliers. The Government could boost the British economy by doing the same.

In order that a 'Buy British' public sector policy does not degenerate into featherbedding, it is necessary that all aid to industry and all public sector purchases from industry are subject to certain conditions. This contract compliance and positive use of public purchasing has been pioneered overseas in countries as diverse as the USA and France. In America defence contracts often contain a clause that a certain proportion of the contract is for research and development expenditure. Other American bodies, such as pension funds and local authorities, often contain equal opportunities clauses in their contracts. French Government agencies have a 'Buy French' policy, sometimes using public contracts as showcases or 'loss-leaders' to develop and promote products for export.

Labour's proposed British National Investment Bank will make most of its lending conditional on the adoption of certain practices by borrowers. A similar policy is already pursued by Labour local authorities.

Operating through the market is one of the ways in which a Labour Government's relationship with industry will differ from that advocated in the past. The problem with the planning agreements of years gone by was that nobody agreed with them and nobody implemented them. A new approach based on the incentive of access to markets – the Marks and Spencer technique – rather than centralised coercion, needs to be tried.

Firms that supply to the public sector will need to adopt best industrial relations practices of employee involvement and consultation. They will have to pay adequate wages, provide proper training and, where appropriate, devote some of the proceeds of Government contracts to research and development. It is economically pointless for the Government to encourage firms to trade down market and worsen conditions of employment and service as has often been the case under the Conservatives. This approach will neither help us to compete with our up market rivals such as Japan, France or Germany nor drag us down fast enough or far enough to compete with the underdeveloped nations.

MR MACGREGOR'S CONJURING TRICKS

As the prospects for the British economy grow increasingly gloomy, the Government's response has been the search for scapegoats and the pathetic claim that (after seven years in office) they must not be blamed for Britain's continued decline – and, of course, desperate attempts to divert attention from these failures. Prominent amongst these attempts have been their distortions about the Labour Party's public expenditure plans. What they have had to say is as economically illiterate as it is politically disreputable. Had it all emanated from Mr Norman Tebbit it would have been no more than we expect. Ritual abuse is his special talent. Dirty tricks are what he is paid for. But the Government has attempted to impose a superficial respectability on their attack on Labour's plans by pretending that Labour's programme has been costed by the Treasury. That pretence was properly corrected by Sir Robert Armstrong, the Cabinet Secretary and Head of the Civil Service. He has written to me to say that the so-called list of spending proposals was drawn up by 'Ministers with the assistance of their political advisers . . . The list of proposals to be costed was not compiled by officials'. The Chief Secretary, John MacGregor, has put his name to the fraud which Ministers and their political advisers have perpetrated.

It is therefore necessary to describe the calculated dishonesty to which he is party. Mr MacGregor lists his hobby in the 1986 Parliamentary Year Book as *conjuring*. So it is not surprising that, with Mr MacGregor, things are not what they seem. After Mr MacGregor pulled the first list of supposedly costed plans out of the hat, I published an item by item exposure of his sleight of hand. Of course, most newspapers chose to ignore it. Yet the respected City analysts Phillips and Drew, along with the National Institute of Economics and Social Studies and the Institute of Fiscal Studies dismissed the MacGregor claims. Subsequently, the *Sunday Times* [12 August 1986] contributed a lie of its own to the Tory campaign. They employed the economic forecasters ITEM to run Mr MacGregor's fraudulent figures through a computer model and then printed the results as proof of the accuracy of his claims. ITEM condemned this distortion. Indeed it specifically denied the *Sunday Times*' claim that they had carried out an independent audit of the MacGregor figures. They stated 'an audit is going through line by line and calculating how much the commitments would cost. We did not do that'. The *Sunday Times* has had neither the courage nor the integrity to print the ITEM statement.

We only need to examine Mr MacGregor's ludicrous claims to understand why Phillips and Drew, ITEM and the Head of the Civil Service all want to dismiss or be distanced from what he is doing. Almost the first rule an aspiring accountant or economist is taught is that you can only add like to like. But Mr MacGregor adds net costs to gross costs to first year costs to full year costs to full programme costs that should be spread over a number of years to costs adjusted for inflation to costs that are unadjusted.

He then rounds his totals up with a good dose of double counting by failing to take account of the savings that flow back to the Treasury from reductions in unemployment. Yet his own Treasury economic model shows that, after three years, increases in capital spending are 32 per cent self-financing and that extra current expenditure on programmes like health and education recoups 47 per cent of their initial cost. Mr MacGregor clearly has no grasp of simple concepts such as timing or the phasing of programmes or the allocation of priorities. To say or to imply that Labour would carry out all of its extra spending at once makes as much a sense as a view that the Tories would carry out their £18 billion privatisation programme overnight. MacGregor makes up figures which contradict the newspaper articles or policy statements he cites as the source of his figures. And he gives other figures which contradict those given by his Tory Party colleagues. He even contradicts himself. Discrepancies of hundreds of millions of pounds divide the costs of some items in the supposed Labour programmes as given in March 1986 and as given in July 1986, despite the fact that the same documents are cited as the source of these policy proposals in both cases.

Included in his list was a figure for the amount of money which Labour will immediately spend on Education. It was, he says, substantiated by a report in the *Guardian* of a speech made by Labour's Education Spokesman. That speech – and the consequent *Guardian* report – contained figures quite different from those in the MacGregor list. A correction was made in Parliament and for a moment Mr MacGregor accepted his mistake in a graceless and grudging admission of his error. Yet, since then, John MacGregor has continued to repeat his claims about the cost of Labour's programme, including the supposed education costs. He still bases these assertions on his discredited list, despite the fact that the many inventions within it have been exposed and explained to him. The original mistakes could have been the product of incompetence. Their repetition, even after they have been identified, can only be described as a lie.

MOTIVES FOR THE TORY DISTORTIONS

Why has Mr MacGregor gone to such extraordinary lengths to distort Labour's policies and in the process destroy what little reputation he had as an Economic Minister – although enhancing his reputation as a conjuror. It is because opinion surveys show two things. The first is that Labour is on course to win the next General Election. The second is that most people would prefer an increase in public expenditure over tax cuts. Indeed in a letter to the *Financial Times* in 1986, John Constable, the BIM's former Director General, stated that

> Repeated surveys of UK managers reveal a clear and strong message that no Government Minister should find difficulty in understanding. In response to his institute's Budget consultation earlier this year, 82 per cent of respondents said they were prepared to forego tax cuts or even pay more in tax to allow for greater spending on hospitals, roads and housing, and 60 per cent to see more spending on education. Only 11 per cent sought cuts in person taxation.

> The reasons for this are straightforward. Two things will certainly prevent continued economic growth: the lack of a modern and adequate infrastructure (which will cost more to repair the longer it deteriorates), and the lack of a skilled and educated workforce [*Financial Times*, 4 July 1986].

The Tories have spent the last seven years telling us that public expenditure is a bad thing. So they will never convince the public between now and the next election, that the prospects for the health service, education, public construction and maintenance, and above all, jobs, are better under them than Labour. Yet it is these very needs that Tory tax cuts will not be able to meet.

The real problem with Mr MacGregor's confidence trick is that policy in neither Government nor opposition is made in the way he tries to imply. No party draws up an arbitrary list of proposals which it seeks to implement in one year regardless of the costs or consequences. I cannot speak for the Conservative Party, but, in the Labour Party, our approach is to set out a firm framework which allows scope for necessary and desirable public expenditure. Our policy statements state that outside our agreed priorities we will only be able to implement policies as and when resources allow. Some of those extra resources will themselves be released by the extra growth and savings that public expenditure will help to generate.

LABOUR'S SPENDING PLANS

Public spending under the next Labour Government will be greater than it is today. That is an economic as well as social necessity. Public spending, at higher levels than today, is necessary to finance the improvements in education and medical care, the increases in house building and the rehabilitation to our infrastructure which are so badly needed and almost universally demanded. Increases in public expenditure are also essential to the recovery of the economy. The sensible policy is a carefully targeted expansion of public sector capital programmes – concentrating investment in areas which are not import sensitive, which produce the most jobs at least cost and which, by their stimulation, stimulate other sectors of the economy.

The increases in public expenditure which are proposed, can – in the short term – be financed by increased borrowing and increased taxation on the top 5 per cent of taxpayers. In the medium-term and long-term, the new policies which are described will be financed in a number of other ways – the increases in Government income which flow from growth, the savings that will follow a reduction in unemployment, the transfer of resources from one programme to another and the encouragement of new forms of investment in Government projects. In the following sections each of these aspects of Labour's spending plans are discussed in more detail.

EXTRA BORROWING

During the 1986 Budget debate we proposed an increase in borrowing of £6 billion – some of it to finance a cut in National Insurance Contributions, most of it to be used for public sector investment and services. That £6 billion figure was the product of a calculation of the borrowing total which would most benefit the economy. We will, of course, replace the meaningless and discredited Public Sector Borrowing Requirement with a public

statement of the ratio of Government debt to national income. At
present the ratio is much lower in Britain than it is in some of our
most successful competitors – Japan, Canada and Italy – and it
would have remained so had borrowing been increased by the £6
billion which we proposed.

Setting a firm financial framework requires the Labour Party to
accept the necessity of accepting a rigorous pattern of priorities.
The Party – and the Trade Unions – have accepted that necessity.
There is a general understanding that parts of our programme will
have to wait for the availability of necessary finance. And there is
widespread agreement that we must not attempt what we cannot
afford or promise what we cannot, prudently, carry out. The
framework which I will set out will not be exceeded.

GROWTH AND UNALLOCATED EXPENDITURE

That does not, of course, mean or imply that in the medium- and
longer-term funds cannot be provided for extra expenditure. It
does mean that it cannot be promised or provided until we know
that the money is there. Apart from the anti-poverty and job
creation programmes which we specify, there can be no promises
for the 'first year'. Other spending programmes have to await the
increased resources which we know are certain to be available. It
is worthwhile remaining ourselves of how they will be provided:

(a) Additional resources will come automatically from economic
    growth. Each 1 per cent of growth provides an extra £1.5
    billion of Government revenue each year for distribution
    between tax cuts and public expenditure. The Government
    anticipated, at the time of their 1986 Budget, that there would
    be a cumulative fiscal adjustment of £9 billion over the three
    years to 1988/9.
(b) In addition, on the Government's own figures, there will be a
    cumulative total of £16.5 billion unallocated expenditure in
    the contingency reserves over the next three years to 1989/90.

Thus, there will be between now and 1989 substantial sums of
unallocated government income – even on the Government's own
calculations. Though it seems likely that they are holding some of
it back for a sudden pre-Election tax cut. I make no complaint
about the Government's refusal to hypothecate its use. The

economic prospect is too uncertain after seven years of Tory policy
– a deteriorating balance of payments, a fragile exchange rate and
over reliance on oil revenues. But some of it will certainly be there
– to be used according to Labour's priorities. What is more, it will
– in time – be augmented by the savings which naturally result
from the reductions in unemployment.

SAVINGS AND THE REALLOCATION OF EXPENDITURE

One of the constant errors of this Government – and of those who
seek to defend it – is the assumption that unemployment has no
cost. In fact the Treasury loses an average of between £6000 and
£7000 – in taxes foregone and benefit paid – for every man and
woman who is out of work. The present level of unemployment
costs the Exchequer £20 billion a year. And £30 billion is
sacrificed in lost production. It is absurd to assume that
unemployment costs nothing whilst job creation is unacceptably
expensive. There was no excuse for that childish mistake. The
Treasury's own model shows that after three years, increases in
capital expenditure are 32 per cent self-financing and that extra
current expenditure on the health and education programmes
recoup 47 per cent of the initial cost. The London Business School
– not instinctive supporters of public spending – put the figures at
75 per cent for capital expenditure and 83 per cent for current
expenditure. Compare the *net cost* of unemployment with the
potential savings on the *gross costs* of public sector employment and
the price we are paying to keep 3½ million men and women out of
work comes into focus.

There are three other savings which justify comment:

(a) In the long term savings must be made in our contribution to
the EEC budget by a radical revision of the Common
Agriculture Policy. The pressures of logic combined with the
tensions created by extended membership, make that
revision certain. One possibility is that the Community
chooses to organise a reasonable regional policy of its own,
which creates jobs in Britain but reduces the savings we can
make in our budget contribution.

(b) There will be a real saving in future years expenditure as a result of the Labour Government heeding the advice given by the National Economic Development Council. By improving the infrastructure in the early years of our Administration we will avoid the ruinous costs of compensating for further dilapidation during the next decade. It is a balance sheet approach to the management of the economy. But it is not an approach which is necessarily reflected in the political credit which we receive during the early, prudent, years.

(c) The Trident Nuclear Weapons system costs over £10 billion. The scrapping of this system will release resources for the maintenance of our non-nuclear contribution to NATO as outlined in the Labour Party's policy document *Defence & Security for Britain* [October 1984].

In addition I have proposed three innovations in order to put public expenditure on a more sensible and efficient footing. The case for a public sector balance sheet is set out in the chapter on Government borrowing [Chapter 5]. Also:

(a) The next Labour Government will need to institute a new system of cash planning. This will not be cash limits of the sort previously operated – which were often set at a level intended to prevent the full implementation of an agreed programme. A new cash planning system must avoid a second shortcoming associated with the present system of cash limits – the choice of hitting targets by cutting programmes (particularly capital expenditure) rather than by improving efficiency. We need to establish some measures by which the performance of spending departments can be assessed so as to determine the efficiency with which they spend their resources. For example, in the health service, cash plans should be set on the basis of such criteria as the length of waiting lists. The Government will then publish both cash plans and the performance-related criteria against which they are measured.

(b) There is a tendency to consider public expenditure in terms of increments on top of present spending levels and programmes. That inevitably results in the continuation of some existing undesirable programmes at the expense of new programmes which have greater value. In Government we should introduce a system of zero based budgeting by which each department is asked periodically to justify all its expenditure, starting from scratch. Emphasis will be given to those areas of expenditure which help reduce unemployment by meeting real needs either in terms of services, or investment or training. Although we propose and emphasise the need for extra public expenditure, our approach is more rigorous than that previously adopted by Oppositions of any party.

THE MOBILISATION OF PRIVATE SECTOR FUNDS

Often private sector sources of finance will put up money if other companies or the public sector will do the same. The local authority enterprise boards have been very successful in pump priming private capital funds. For every one pound of public money supplied by the enterprise boards, one to three pounds of private capital has been mobilised. For example, the West Midland Enterprise Board has set up a unit trust which they jointly manage alongside Lazard Brothers Merchant Bank. This has raised £4.25 million of pension fund money for investment in the West Midlands.

The National Investment Bank will also be looking for joint ventures with both private institutions and the local enterprise boards, particularly in order to put together packages of long-term or soft-loan finance.

Soft-loan Government finance or guarantees available over substantial periods of time are also increasingly essential if our industry is to be in a position to compete with companies from Japan, Germany and France who take such aid for granted when they tender for major overseas capital projects.

The Bosphorous Bridge contract was lost and the building of the Channel Tunnel delayed because of the absence of adequate Government guarantees.

Many private jobs and substantial private investment depend on public guarantees. It is simply foolish not to maintain or mobilise such resources. Whatever our ideological position we cannot play the *laissez-faire* game when our international rivals are playing by a different rule book.

TAXATION

There should be a further source of additional revenue that will allow an increase in one specific area of public expenditure. An anti-poverty programme involving an increase in state pensions, child benefit and improved benefits for the long-term unemployed, costs something around £3.6 billion. By design that is the sum of the total tax reductions which have been enjoyed during the last seven years by the highest paid 5 per cent of wage and salary earners and receivers of capital income, gains and transfers. Thus Labour proposes a discrete tax and benefit package, an intentional and carefully circumscribed exercise in redistribution. Whilst a small and advantaged group have had their taxes cut, for the rest of the working population taxes have increased under the Conservatives. A tax policy which takes more from the average and low income groups and less from the richest twentieth of society is fundamentally wrong. I am not in favour of high taxes in principle. But cutting the taxes of the richest 5 per cent was not a discrete choice and should not have been a priority. It had unavoidable consequences – amongst them the reduction in the quality of social and public services that were required to allow the expenditure savings by which the tax cuts were financed. That is not acceptable to me and I do not intend to prevaricate about Labour's intention to help the poor. The highly paid – and I am one of them – will have to contribute more. It is superstition and self-interest not hard evidence which prompts the argument that overall economic performance will deteriorate as a result.

The Conservatives attempt to justify a reduction in top tax rates by claiming that it provides added incentive for those at the top of the income scale. Indeed they have already argued that a reduction in tax rates actually increases the tax income from those on the highest income. That is palpable nonsense. Recent increases in the percentage of revenue collected from those in the highest tax brackets are not the results of lower marginal rates. They are the product of a widening divergence between the primary earnings of the rich and the primary earnings of the rest. The Treasury's own figures show that the earnings of the top 10 per cent of men rose seven times as fast as those of the bottom 10 per cent. This divergence has little or nothing to do with the incentive effect of lower tax rates. It was not lower tax rates that prompted the Chairmen of recently privatised industries to increase their salaries. Nor are they working any harder. The massive salaries now paid in the City are in no way related to tax cuts. To justify lower taxes as a way to ensure that the rich help the poor is transparent hypocrisy – greed dressed up to look like benevolence.

Before we can think of tax cuts in general we have to ensure that the wealthiest 5 per cent pay their proper share. The wealthiest 5 per cent are individuals on incomes of £20 000 p.a. or more – not families but individuals. As well as being undesirable it is virtually impossible to fix tax rates for family income. When, as we intend, income is disaggregated for tax purposes it will be literally impossible.

In requiring the richest 5 per cent to pay their proper contribution towards the national budget; I do not intend to return to very high marginal rates such as 98 per cent – a percentage which virtually no-one paid. Our policies will concern the average effective rate of tax which is actually paid by the highest income recipients. That means:

1. Limiting items currently allowable against the marginal tax rate so that the allowance is only calculated against the standard rate.
2. Removing the ceiling from employees' national insurance contribution which, as it presently operates, requires a man or woman on £65 or £165 a week to make a contribution on every pound of income whilst nothing is paid on any pound above £265 a week. This would raise £600 million per annum.
3. Another category of income, which is mainly received by the better off and is also exempt from National Insurance contribution, is income obtained from investment rather than from working. The next Labour Government must examine the case for the continuation of such exemptions. There should, of course, be a minimum figure below which the earnings from savings would be exempt from National Insurance contributions – thus protecting small savers. Already, following the removal of the ceiling on employer National Insurance contributions, firms are looking to avoid National Insurance by paying their employees in ways that do not attract the levy. This loophole must be closed down.
4. The yield from the taxation of capital and wealth must be

increased. Capital taxes now provide 1 per cent of the total tax
paid. In 1908 the figure was 29 per cent, in 1948, 9 per cent.
Clearly we need wealth and capital gains taxes to take a fairer
share of the total tax burden. The taxation of capital gains
must be progressive and the loopholes which allowed such
avoidance must be closed.

5. A tightening of tax loopholes which allow the better off
   (intentionally and with the assistance of highly paid advisers)
   to escape paying their proper share of Exchequer income.

One of the problems of the British taxation system is that half the
total income earned in our economy is not taxed at all. Because of
the large number of allowances and the vast amount of tax
avoidance and evasion, tax which is levied at source from wage
earners (usually on modest incomes) contributes more than its
proper share of Government revenue. Remuneration – whether in
the form of cash or other benefits – should normally be taxed on an
equivalent basis. There may be some cases when the tax system
has to be used ingeniously to protect British industry and create
British jobs. But too often in the past, benefits have been valued at
an artificially favourable rate – giving a real advantage to those
higher income earners who can choose between cash and kind.
Knowing the opportunity for misrepresentation in this area, let
me repeat that the examination of allowances which I propose in
no way affects the clear promise we have made to retain tax relief
on mortgage interest at the standard rate.

5 Government Borrowing*

CONSERVATIVE CRITICISMS OF GOVERNMENT BORROWING

Any Government should take a prudent view of Government borrowing. But it is wholly wrong to suggest that prudent borrowing is the same as slavish adherence to the rules laid down by the Conservative Government for compliance with the arbitrary targets they have set for the public sector borrowing requirement (PSBR) – not least because the PSBR is, itself, such an inadequate measurement. We need something better. In this chapter the indicators that the next Labour Government will use as the basis of our borrowing policy are set out. No-one doubts the need for the use of such indicators. Our argument with the Government concerns the absurd way in which the targets for these indicators have been set.

The Government and its supporters have, on occasion, made at least four different criticisms of Government borrowing – any Government borrowing:

1. It crowds out alternative and superior investment by using limited resources for low utility projects.
2. It so increases the demand for investment finance that it pushes up interest rates.
3. It bequeaths a legacy of debt to future generations.
4. It can be inflationary – in particular because of the links between increases in the PSBR and the money supply.

As a result of one or more of these problems it is claimed that borrowing is damaging to the economy and does not generate employment. Each of these contentions needs critical examination.

First, on resource crowding out, it is unacceptable to imply that investment by the NUM pension fund in the Washington Watergate complex is, in any way, superior to investment in the new Selby Coalfield just because the former is private sector and

---

* Based on speech to Financial Times Conference on the 'City Revolution', London, 12 July 1986.

the latter is public sector. If there is a problem of crowding out, it is important for projects like Selby not to be crowded out by Watergate – or forced to pay high interest rates because competing investment opportunities pay more. Resource crowding out can only take place in an economy approaching full employment of resources. The idea that a public sector infrastructure programme is somehow competing for resources with the private sector is ludicrous at a time when construction firms and direct labour organisations are chronically underutilised and there are as many as 400 000 unemployed construction workers on the dole. Certainly the CBI and the construction industry, consistently lobbying for more infrastructure expenditure, do not believe in the dangers of crowding out. They want the Government to borrow more so that the nation is 'crowded in' to work.

'Crowding out' is therefore a catch-phrase that ought to be kept in proper perspective. British money still floods abroad. Building societies are awash with funds. Retained company earnings have increased sharply. A moderate increase in public borrowing will not deny investment funds to private industry. It will, however, provide them for the public sector. The case for an increase in public borrowing is overwhelming – so long as it is used to promote investment in, and demand for, the products of British industry.

Borrowing to finance investment is normal practice in private industry. Borrowing is not sinful. Indeed, if it is well used for sensible purposes, it is a highly desirable – and wholly unexceptional – way of paying for new plant and machinery. The famous Grantham grocer's shop was probably bought on credit. At least in this particular, what is good for Thatcher's family business is good for Britain.

Second, financial crowding out. It is difficult to justify the contention that public sector borrowing has to be held down in order to keep interest rates low. That was the argument of the first two years of this Government's life. The argument then changed to the insistence that British interest rates were high because of the competing rates offered by the economies of other developed countries – America in particular. That explanation has been abandoned with the fall in American interest rates and the increase in British rates. It is now tacitly accepted by the Government that base rate is partly determined by the Treasury and held at its present record level in order to prevent downward pressure on the pound.

The truth is that interest rates are determined by a whole host of variables besides Government borrowing, some of which are beyond immediate Government control. These include inflation expectations, international interest rates, the level of private borrowing and the total level of Government debt that needs to be financed. Thus, despite cuts in the PSBR and in the ratio of Government debt to GDP, under the Conservatives real interest rates are the highest in living memory. The evidence from both the USA and the UK is that there is no systematic inverse relationship between definitions of the budget deficit such as PSBR and interest rates.

Third, although it is true that borrowing does affect the level of outstanding public sector debt, it is wrong to assert that this is invariably damaging or undesirable. Much of the second half of this chapter will be concerned with setting out criteria by which the desirability or otherwise of debt can be established.

Finally the possible inflationary effects of borrowing depend on the ability of the supply-side of the economy to respond to a fiscal stimulus. Obviously, this is likely to be more of a problem in a buoyant economy. If there is spare capacity there is no reason why expansion should be inflationary provided that appropriate supporting monetary and other policies are pursued.

The danger is that, in setting crude intermediate targets for borrowing or the money supply, the Government ends up unintentionally adjusting the entire economy in order to hit these targets, rather than directly regulating these variables in order to achieve certain final objectives for the real economy. That is exactly what this Government has done.

PROBLEMS WITH THE PSBR

If crude antipathy to public borrowing is generally misplaced, then, in the UK, this problem is compounded by the bizarre and unique statistic that we use to measure borrowing – namely the PSBR. Added to our difficulties is the odd way in which the present Government has chosen to manipulate and interpret the PSBR statistic.

The problem of the PSBR and PSBR targeting has seven elements:

1. Asset sales.
2. The inclusion of some nationalised industries but not others.
3. The absence of a clear distinction between capital maintenance and current expenditures.
4. The fact that variations in the PSBR do not give a good guide to the public sector's net worth – i.e., what is happening to the balance of public sector assets and public sector liabilities, both real and financial.
5. The suppression of built-in fiscal stabilisers – in other words not allowing the PSBR to adjust to and dampen the cycle as tax revenues and welfare expenditures vary in response to variations in the level of economic activity.
6. The absence of inflation adjustments.
7. Finally, it is impossible to get sensible information about borrowing if use is made of only one statistic to convey a variety of different sorts of information. Even then, in the opinion of the Institute of Fiscal Studies, an 'inflation-adjusted, capital-adjusted, depletion-related, pension-sensitive PSBR would not be a very good guide'.

The real issue facing any Government is a level of public borrowing which is *consistent with* and which *contributes to* its other economic aims. The error of the present Government has been the almost mystical belief that by setting targets for the money supply and the PSBR, the sort of economy which they hoped to create would *automatically* result. That mechanical result has clearly not emerged. What is worse, it has prompted the Government into taking a whole swathe of decisions which, welfare aside, are patently bad for the economy. A typical example is the disposal – at artificially low prices – of appreciating public assets. Undoubtedly one of the underlying reasons for the sale of British Telecom has been in order to fulfil ideological aims. Their sales are, in part, the product of the unsubstantiated belief that their efficiency will increase in the private sector. But it was chiefly done to finance tax cuts – the sacrifice of Government capital in the interest of Government revenue. It is especially hard to argue that holding down public sector borrowing is concerned with the reduction of the debts which future generations will inherit. In actual fact, the reverse is true. For what is happening is the run down of Government assets with no matching reduction in Government liabilities. The Government is using asset sale proceeds to reduce taxation, not borrowing.

If the Government's privatisation programme remains on course it has been estimated that lost profits and reduced income tax receipts could eventually amount to £5.5 billion per annum. The tax cuts financed by asset sales are only sustainable so long as there is a continuing flow of income from those assets. Once the sale of assets dries up, so does that particular means to finance tax reductions, with the result that either taxes will have to go up again or public expenditure will have to be cut. A not dissimilar process is occurring with the disposal of non-renewable oil and gas deposits. Even at their peak in 1985 the £12 billion per annum revenues from North Sea oil and gas only covered the increase in the total annual Exchequer cost of unemployment. Again, instead of the oil bonus being used to build-up future assets, it has been frittered away.

The Government's argument for keeping nationalised industry borrowing within the PSBR are wholly spurious. Apart from concern with crowding out, it is claimed that nationalised industry borrowing is legitimately listed as Government debt because it bears a Government guarantee. That is patently untrue. The Government did not bail out the Mersey Docks and Harbour Board – despite the inclusion of its debt within the PSBR – whilst on more than one occasion the Government has bailed out private sector companies and banks. In any event, companies supported by the Government incur debts which are underwritten by the Treasury, but are not included within the PSBR. Moreover, there is an arbitrary distinction between some state companies whose borrowing enters into the PSBR and others whose borrowing does not. If the British Railways Board borrows on the private market to finance investment, this borrowing increases the PSBR. If British Leyland – also owned by the Government – borrows on the private market, this borrowing has no effect on the PSBR. Of course, nationalised industries cannot be left free to borrow what they choose – irrespective of Government policy. They should be required to respond to criteria laid down by the Treasury and their sponsoring department. But the general criterion ought to be the well-being of the industries within the general development of the economy.

Another problem stems from the planning of all Government

spending in cash terms with no clear distinction between capital spending and current spending, and, within current spending, between capital maintenance and other forms of expenditure. In order to hit what amount to arbitrary PSBR targets, capital and capital maintenance expenditure has usually been squeezed regardless of the virtue of funding such expenditure by borrowing. Thus, often public sector companies or capital programmes have seen their borrowing restricted in a way which would not have applied to enterprises within the private sector. External Finance Limits in industries such as gas and electricity have been manipulated as a form of hidden taxation. British Telecom has more leeway over borrowing now because it has been transferred to the private sector. But that is not an argument for privatisation. It is an argument for sensible public accounting and a more rational approach to borrowing.

Governments through the years have – in fact – been far from profligate in their overall borrowing. It is worth noting that although the Government uses credit for a range of different purposes, it does not use it to finance current services. Apart from the years of war, current services have always cost less than current taxation. The Government borrows to invest – in housing, in construction and in a variety of projects which would be financed in the same way were they in the private rather than the public sector.

The worst example of arbitrary limits on borrowing having an adverse effect on taxpayers and the economy alike was brought out in the NEDO report – *Investment in the Public Sector Built Infrastructure*. This catalogued a list of up to £15 billion worth of necessary infrastructure repairs and maintenance. The implication was that, unless work was started now, the costs would escalate with consequent higher tax burdens on future generations. Although borrowing to finance repairs would increase public sector debt, the net finance repairs would increase public sector debt, the net effect of work carried out now rather than later would be a saving. Such important considerations are lost in the present Government's obsession with the PSBR. If the effects of public spending on the value of public sector capital assets were presented more clearly it would be apparent that the justification for cuts in capital and maintenance spending must be made in terms of current economic policy alone, not in appeals to notions of prudent regard for future taxpayers.

Problems associated with the inclusion in the PSBR of investment by nationalised industries, or the sale of public assets, would be solved by a switch to a measure such as general Government financial deficit. But targeting such a variable – indeed any fixed, nominal definition of borrowing – entails the abandonment of the automatic fiscal stabilisers. So, by setting a rigid target, the tendency of taxes to fall and welfare payments to rise as demand and employment fall, is offset. The effect is that the initial fall in activity is reinforced. Since this is highly undesirable, there is a strong argument for allowing fiscal stabilisers to operate. There are certainly problems in trying to offset small, short-run variations in demand by additional discretionary 'fine-tuning' of the level of Government spending or taxation. But it is simply untrue to say that 'coarse-tuning' in response to larger, more broad-based variations in demand is either impossible or undesirable. The evidence from both the USA and the UK is overwhelming. Variations in the level of activity are partly related to variations in a suitably adjusted measure of the Government's budget deficit.

Given that the Government *has* to make a decision about the level of borrowing, it is best that this is done on a systematic basis taking account, to the best of its ability, of underlying realities. The problem with setting crude targets is that they hide reality; and because they mislead they make planning harder not easier. For example, although the nominal PSBR in both 1981/2 and 1982/3 remained the same at £9 billion, the IFS has calculated that this figure was associated with an increase in public sector net financial liabilities in the first year of £3.3 billion but a decrease in net liabilities of £9.1 billion in the following year.

The PSBR, as presently constructed and applied, contains no mechanism for inflation adjustment. Inflation operates like a tax – reducing the public sector's net liabilities. Thus, because of inflation during the post war period, the real value of the national debt has steadily fallen even though year by year the Government borrowing requirement has been positive. In real terms Government borrowing has not saddled Britain with an unbearable burden of debt. Indeed, when the PSBR is adjusted for inflation it becomes apparent that over the past 20 years the effects have been far more contractionary than the nominal figures would suggest.

The chief problem with the PSBR, or any other single measure of Government borrowing that is targeted, is that it is taken as an indicator of too many different things. These include:

1. A measure of fiscal policy stance.
2. A decrease in the public sector's net worth.
3. The supposed scope for tax cuts.
4. An indicator for financial policy, particularly in relation to interest rates and the money supply. Implicit within this is the view that it is also an indicator of the Government's anti-inflationary stance.

A satisfactory set of indicators for borrowing must pay regard to all four of these tasks. And so, despite all the superstitions and misconceptions, it is not possible – and it never will be possible – to treat the control of public borrowing lightly. A convincing borrowing policy is essential to the maintenance of international confidence. It is also a necessary framework within which to build our plans for growth and reduced unemployment. Stating some form of nominal borrowing framework – and stating it in a way which confirms the Government's determination to adhere to it – gives a signal to this and to competitor economies about the prudent management of the economy.

AN ALTERNATIVE FRAMEWORK

My approach to public finance will revolve around two sets of published figures. First, a public sector balance sheet will be published which will show the implication of public expenditure and borrowing decisions for public sector liabilities and public sector assets both real and financial. Second, discipline towards borrowing will be carried out with reference to the general Government debt–output ratio.

Within the Treasury our fiscal stance will be set with reference to a third set of figures – the general Government financial deficit. Inflation-adjusted and cyclically-adjusted versions of the general Government financial deficit will also need to inform our policy. Inflation-adjusted figures are necessary in order to take account of the possible demand effects of a decline in the real value of Government debt due to inflation. Cyclically-adjusted figures are needed in order to help distinguish the appropriate level of discretionary demand stimulation from the operation of built-in fiscal stabilisers. Such indicators are only really of use if we consider their movement through time, and relative to GDP, in the context of the economic models we use to help us set policy. The general Government financial deficit will not be targeted. However, it will be taken into account when setting the pre-announced guidelines embodied in the public sector balance sheet and the ratio of general Government debt to GDP.

The IFS has put the case for a public sector balance sheet eloquently and is worth quoting in full:

> Imagine that the Managing Director of a major company stands up at the annual shareholders' meeting and presents the year's results and plans for the coming year in terms of a single number, the size of the company's borrowing. He gives no figures for the company's existing borrowing or other liabilities and gives little indication of what the borrowing will be used for in terms of capital investment or covering a current deficit. Nor does he state new liabilities other than new borrowing. Even in the company accounts there is no balance sheet to say whether the company's net worth is increasing or diminishing. There is a figure for gross investment but none for depreciation of existing assets. Given this paucity of information it is hardly surprising that there are no inflation-adjusted current cost accounts and no breakdown of the company's domestic and international position. Despite all this he congratulates himself on his prudent housekeeping and on the tight financial disciplines which have been imposed by the company.
>
> It is unlikely that such a Managing Director would carry much authority with the shareholders, that the accounts would be accepted as a true, fair or remotely adequate statement of the company's position or that the Stock Exchange would allow quotation of its shares. And yet this is of course a description of the information contained in the Chancellor's annual Budget Statement and the accompanying Red Book (Financial Statement and Budget Report) with their overwhelming emphasis on the Public Sector Borrowing Requirement (PSBR) [IFS, *Public Finances in Perspective*, Report No. 8, February 1984, p. 5].

My intention, therefore, is to publish a public sector balance sheet in order to provide information and reassurance to the City and public opinion alike. Such a balance sheet can be constructed from existing Government statistical resources. The methodology is not new. It has been developed by academics such as Prof Willem Buiter and institutions such as the IFS. The balance sheet will show public sector assets balanced against public sector liabilities with the difference measuring net worth. Such a balance sheet will present a number of advantages and a number of disciplines.

First, it will put public sector and private company borrowing to finance investment on a similar footing. *The same criteria will apply to all potentially productive Government investment.* If the net worth of the housing stock, the roads and airports increases, then – all other economic considerations being equal – the government should not stand in the way of the borrowing, anymore than it would stand in the way of borrowing by ICI, Marks and Spencer or GEC. The aim is to ensure that the public sector does not miss out on prudent or profitable investment opportunities merely because of the arbitrary and unsatisfactory nature of present public accounting conventions. The present Government seems to have forgotten that under certain circumstances it *is* responsible to borrow to finance investment.

Second, the profligacy of using asset sales to finance tax cuts, neglecting infrastructure repairs with consequent costs for future taxpayers and running down oil reserves without using the proceeds to invest in other wealth generating assets, would all become far more explicit under the balance sheet approach. Posing behind the facade of tight curbs on borrowing the present Conservative Government has in fact been both profligate and irresponsible.

Third, by spelling out in detail the implications of Government expenditure programmes, it will be less easy for Governments – either wittingly or unwittingly – to sanction an excessive tax burden on future generations.

The more immediate macro-economic effects of Government borrowing are best monitored by reference to the ration of outstanding general Government financial debt to GDP. The limit which is placed – by reference to that index – on public borrowing has to be determined by the needs of the real economy. The principal object of the next Labour Government will be a revitalisation of the economy and a consequent reduction in unemployment. There will be a level of Government debt which, being exceeded, will hamper that process – as there will be a level of Government debt which is necessary to proceed towards our goal at maximum speed.

The level of Government debt will *not* be a residual element in our economic planning. It will be an essential interlocking element. But it will not be an objective which is pursued irrespective of the consequences for the real economy. To ignore the total volume of Government borrowing, as was once Treasury practice, is clearly foolish. The same can be said about disregard of the money supply. *But obsessive preoccupation with government borrowing and the money supply – particularly when reinforced with the pretence that a target can be determined which, if achieved, will set the economy on the road to recovery – is simply futile.* The obsession with the PSBR target is particularly futile when we know, from the experience of the last six years, that it is self defeating. Cutting the PSBR in the pursuit of an arbitrary target has fiscal and social consequences which simply increase the PSBR in other ways.

As a guideline I will announce an objective for the debt–GDP ratio. However, my main concern will be with its underlying long-term trend. This will help reassure the markets that they will not be expected to absorb an unacceptably high amount of debt with consequent adverse effects on interest rates. The expenditure proposals which we suggested for the 1986/7 financial year required a small growth in the ratio of debt to GDP. That figure is modest by comparison with what has been common in Britain under Governments of both parties since the war and is certainly smaller than the debt–output ratio found in some of our more successful competitors – Japan, Canada and Italy.

Guidelines about the debt–income ratio, however, offer no assurances about inflation. Indeed, since higher inflation tends to lower this ratio, thus warranting a more expansionary fiscal policy, this guideline by itself gives a perverse indication about the appropriate response of fiscal policy to inflation. I have made it clear that inflation will not be allowed to rise to levels that undermine the credibility of Labour's economic policy or threaten our aim to boost output and employment. There is no advantage to our jobs package in letting inflation get out of hand. Indeed, high and rising inflation only necessitates the slowdown of growth and is therefore damaging to our jobs programme.

Government borrowing does not exist in itself or for itself. The next Labour Government will make decisions about the real economy it hopes to create – the reduction in unemployment which is possible, the level of inflation which is tolerable. That will require us to make judgements about the interest and exchange rates which will best serve those ends. In turn that will oblige us to take account of those money supply and borrowing indicators which contribute to our central aims. The borrowing level is a contribution to policy, not a policy in itself. The current heresy is to treat it as if it had a life and meaning of its own. For us such indicators are a means by which to guide our policy as we attempt to hit our targets for real variables such as growth and employment.

6 Exchange Rates and Exchange Controls*

THE BALANCE OF PAYMENTS BACKGROUND

A currency crisis, which would normally and inevitably follow as balance of payments difficulties loom was only held back in early 1987 by a combination of the highest real interest rates in our history (and in the developed world) and a number of fortuitious circumstances that cannot last – an OPEC price increase, chaos inside the EMS and dollar weakness. Nevertheless sterling still fell to its lowest ever level against the Deutschmark.

The Government admits that the balance of payments will be in deficit in 1987 by £1.5 billion. None of the independent forecasters believe that estimate accurately to represent the extent of the deficit. They estimate that it would be between £2.3 billion and £3.4 billion. The balance of manufactured trade will deteriorate from a surplus of £4.5 billion in 1981 to a deficit of £7.5 billion in 1987 – even on the Government's estimate. That decline will come about at a time when manufacturing exports should have been filling the gap inevitably left by decreasing production of North Sea oil. Anyone who doubts either these predictions, or the seriousness of the problem they pose, should judge the Government's own record. In 1986 at the time of the budget, we were promised a balance of payments surplus of £3.5 billion and the Chancellor boasted that we had adjusted to the reduction in oil revenues without appreciable damage. Eight months later that forecast was substantially revised down to break even.

There is no honest dispute about the reason for the disappearance of our trade surplus. Because of the damage done to manufacturing industry by Government policy, it can no longer keep pace with the demand for manufactured goods. For example, motor imports increased by 15.25 per cent between the third quarter of 1985 and the third quarter of 1986. Other consumer

* Based on speech to Teeside Fabians, Middlesbrough, 13 January 1985; speech to Bond Club of London, 4 November 1985; speech to Institutional Investors Conference, New York, 11 September 1986; speech to General Federation of Trade Unions, Manchester, 15 October 1986.

goods imports increased by 19.5 per cent. The demand for imported goods has escalated as a direct result of the explosion in consumer debt and earnings which outstrip the rise in inflation – a situation which Nigel Lawson condemns in the House of Commons but about which Norman Tebbit boasted in a Party Political broadcast. According to the Governor of the Bank of England, the ratio of household debt to household income has risen to 70 per cent – as compared with 45 per cent during the disastrous and discredited Barber credit boom of 1973. We are wholly unprepared for the reduction in oil revenues. The surplus in our balance of trade in oil will more than halve from £8 billion in 1985 to £3.5 billion in 1987. We have totally failed to use the revenues received, at the peak of oil production, to prepare the economy for that change. The idea that invisible earnings – the product of the expansion in our financial institutions – can fill the gap is clearly the product of either wishful thinking or vested interest.

In short we are facing a credit and consumption boom of unparalleled proportions with which the domestic economy is wholly unable to cope. Against this background there can be no possible justification for cutting taxation, increasing consumption, encouraging more consumer debt, sucking in more imports and both bringing nearer, and making more certain, a balance of trade and sterling crisis.

THE LIMITS TO EXCHANGE RATE ADJUSTMENT

To make up for the run down of North Sea oil revenues it will be necessary to increase our non-oil exports. The structural shift will not be easy or smooth. Whilst we work to achieve the necessary adjustment. Britain's high marginal propensity to import will increase the risk that any improvement in the rate of economic growth will destroy our balance of payments current account – unless we take positive action to protect it.

The conventional answer to the balance of payments constraint – indeed one of the conventional techniques for increasing employment – is an adjustment in the exchange rate. Of course, we need an exchange rate which encourages exports rather than assists imports. And some adjustment in the value of sterling may therefore be necessary – at least against the weighted average of currencies. But we would be unwise to place all our faith in that single remedy.

- Only part of the performance of British exports – and the problem of import penetration – is the result of price competition. Softening the market by sterling depreciation will not encourage improved quality, delivery and service.
- In the past, devaluations have fed through to prices and wages so that any real competitive advantage has been quickly eroded by higher inflation. Although a tough prices policy and an agreement on incomes may help to avoid this problem, undue adjustment of the exchange rate may overstrain such arrangements.
- We cannot assume that a devaluation will not be met by similar measures overseas so that a beggar-my-neighbour spiral of exchange rate adjustment ensues. The Labour Party is not and cannot be a party of perpetual devaluation.

INTERNATIONAL CO-ORDINATION AND IMPORT CONTROLS

Of course, the ideal solution is a co-ordinated international expansion. But it is also the most difficult solution to achieve. In technical terms a generally agreed increase in world demand is a way to raise the size of the multiplier and thus reduce the balance of payments constraint on expansion. The next Labour Government will work for such a solution and will be assisted in its pursuit by like-minded foreign Governments. The IMF attempts to solve the world banking crisis by reducing economic activity in the debtor nations. The EEC resolutely refuses to discuss European economic expansion. The Conservative Government encourages inertia and complacency. A Labour Government will advocate co-ordination for growth. But we would be foolish either to rely on the achievement of co-ordinated expansion or depress ourselves with the fear that single nation recovery is impossible. Without co-operation from other Governments reflation will be more difficult. But it will still be possible.

Unless we can take part in a co-ordinated reflation of world trade Britain may be forced to hold back imports. We could not sit back, unprotected, while other Governments operate policies which both maintain high levels of unemployment in their domestic economies and export their deflation to Britain. The international recession is the worst of all beggar-my-neighbour trade policies. Any Government which – like the Thatcher administration here in Britain – deepens the international depression does far more to inhibit trade than any reasonably applied policy of import limitation. I repeat, action on imports is certainly a second-best solution. But unless and until there is a co-ordinated international reflation we will have to protect ourselves against inadequate demand in the monetarist economies simply producing a massive increase in our imports but no extra jobs within the United Kingdom.

With or without import controls, in conditions of general world deflation our imports are certain to be at a lower figure than that which our trading partners would wish. Imports may be held back by our deepening recession. Or they may be held back by controls which allow us to grow more prosperous despite the general international climate. In any event, the controls we propose would have nothing like the damaging effect on world trade as that which would result from another instalment of calculated deflation intended to force the PSBR and the money supply back into line. But any scheme for limiting imports should be seen as an essentially temporary expedient neither enough in itself to solve the problems nor capable of providing a permanent solution.

Both the adjustment in the exchange rate and the limitation on the rate of growth in imports need augmentation by direct government action:

– Public sector purchasing must be concentrated much more directly on British goods with central and local government and nationalised industries using their powers as bulk buyers to ensure that British producers supply goods at a price and quality which competes with foreign imports [see Chapter 4].
– The fiscal boost to the economy which we propose must be concentrated on higher public expenditure, not lower taxes. And the increases in public expenditure – when they are not a direct contribution to additional employment – must be directed towards capital expenditure rather than consumption [see Chapter 4].

NO RETURN TO STATUTORY EXCHANGE CONTROLS

Because of the importance to industry of stable and competitive exchange rates and because of Britain's special position as a world financial centre we must take a specific and realistic view on the position of sterling.

The Labour Party has no intention of reintroducing statutory exchange controls. There will be no legal prohibition on the export of capital from the United Kingdom economy. We have taken that decision for a number of reasons. Statutory exchange controls prior to 1979 were administered by hundreds of people working in the Bank of England. The Conservatives dispersed these people and shredded their records. The pre-1979 regime grew increasingly less effective as Government became less keen and less able to enforce it in the face of the City's ability to circumvent it. Certainly it did not prevent the exchange rate crisis in 1976. And statutory controls did not save the French Socialist Government from persistent exchange rate crisis in their early years despite the added back up of membership of the EMS. The ability of exchange controls in open trading economies like the UK to hold out against mobile, largely private, international capital flows is severely over-rated.

The conclusion drawn by some is that any new statutory regime would have to be more comprehensive and more vigorously enforced than the pre-1979 regime. The trouble is that such a regime could not be put in place overnight in order to catch the markets by surprise in the morning – not least because the currency markets operate around the world 24 hours a day and can shift billions of pounds out of sterling in seconds at the flick of a button.

The threat to impose statutory controls could actually provoke, not prevent, an exchange rate crisis. Speculators would drive money out of sterling before the election date in order to avoid exchange controls.

A more controversial reason for opposing statutory exchange controls is the damage they would do to City earnings. There is much wrong with the way the City operates, not least its detachment from the fortunes of the domestic economy and its obsession with short-term returns. But currently the City contributes net overseas earnings of £7.6 billion to the balance of payments compared to a manufacturing deficit of over £4 billion and a surplus of £4.0 billion from oil – a figure that is down from £8.0 billion in 1985. Manufacturing already has to substantially improve its position in order to make up for the declining contribution of oil. That is just about feasible with a determined industrial strategy over a number of years. But if it has to make up not only for the run-down of oil earnings but also the run down of City earnings as well, then the balance of payments constraint on growth and the reduction of unemployment becomes even more severe. Although the purpose of statutory controls would presumably be to increase our room for manoeuvre, the indirect effect would be the opposite.

A MODERN SUBSTITUTE FOR STATUTORY CONTROL

As the capitalist system becomes more sophisticated so must the socialist response. That is why the 1985 Labour Party Conference passed a resolution in favour of a new, modern non-statutory form of tax-based exchange control. The way this will work is that managed funds – pension funds, insurance funds, unit trusts and investment trusts – would lose their tax concessions if they held more than a specified proportion of their investment portfolio overseas. The tax concessions available are so substantial that the threat of their removal will be sufficient to not only discourage further capital outflows but also induce the repatriation to the UK of some of the assets held overseas. This would put upward pressure on the exchange rate allowing a Labour Government to hold interest rates at a lower rate than would otherwise be the case.

There can be no doubt about the need to exert downward pressure on interest rates. Real interest rates in the UK now stand at their highest level in history. Indeed they are twice the US level.

Excessive real interest rates are damaging in five ways. First, they choke the demand for investment. Second, they add to industry's costs – e.g., the CBI calculates that a 1 per cent rise in interest rates adds £400 million to costs. Third, interest charges are an unproductive burden on public expenditure. Since 1976 interest payments have grown, even though productive expenditure has been cut. Fourth, high interest rates have resulted in periods of over-valuation of sterling, with damaging consequences for the competitiveness of British industry. Fifth, high mortgage rates feed through to the retail price index thereby fuelling wage pressure. By acting on that part of the City over which a UK government does have control the expectations of the rest of the City are affected without threatening their earning power in the UK. Thus we get some of the advantages of exchange controls without the problems that a reimposition of statutory controls would cause.

It must be admitted that although I originally floated the proposal for a tax-based alternative to exchange control alongside plans for a National Investment Bank the linking of these two proposals has caused unnecessary confusion with some people believing that the primary purpose of repatriation was that it should act as a source of funding for the NIB. The case for our scheme which replaces exchange control and the case for a British National Investment Bank each stand in their own right. If we are to reduce the level of unemployment as our first priority Britain needs a replacement for exchange control as an extra lever for exchange rate policy. Similarly there is no doubt that we need a long-term lending institution specifically directed to the regeneration of industry, regardless of whether or not we had our repatriation incentive scheme.

Before the abolition of statutory exchange control, on average, about 5 per cent of institutional funds were invested abroad. This now amounts to over 16 per cent. Our general objective will be to reduce the percentage to something like the 1979 figure, though there would clearly be a transitional period and we would not intend to treat every institution according to the same rigid formula. Our proposals neither affect direct overseas investment by British companies, nor holiday makers and businessmen wanting to take small sums out of the country. Nor do they affect inward investment flows whether direct or portfolio. We can find examples of similar policies if we look overseas. The Japanese and the French place limitations on outflows of indirect investment. And Canadian law in certain provinces leaves pension funds with a choice. Either they invest a certain proportion in the province or they lose tax advantages.

EXCHANGE CONTROL AND CAPITAL FLOWS

Exchange control was removed in 1979, partly for ideological reasons, but partly to allow an outflow of capital and thus ensure that sterling did not become even more overvalued. The North Sea oil surplus had to go somewhere the Conservatives said. The argument here was that there was no alternative to the removal of exchange control in 1979. An alternative policy which would have been pursued by Labour would have been to run the domestic economy at a higher growth rate with higher rates of domestic rather than foreign investment and lower levels of UK unemployment. We would have used North Sea oil to build up domestic industry rather than allowing its impact on the exchange rate to accelerate the decline of our industry. The result of higher domestic investment, employment and growth would have been a much smaller balance of payments surplus, a much less undervalued pound in the early 1980s and a much stronger longer term competitive position for the economy as a whole. Adopting policies which encouraged the private bonus from North Sea to flow into foreign rather than domestic investment, and which used North Sea tax revenues to pay for the two million extra unemployed that resulted from low domestic investment, has meant that the Conservatives have wasted the opportunity given to the UK by North Sea oil.

The justification for our proposals for repatriation is in part the mirror image of the Conservative justification for allowing a substantial outflow of capital abroad. The repatriation of a percentage of institution overseas portfolios will exert some upward pressure on sterling values. And it will help to avert any over-depreciation which would undermine our efforts to rebuild British industry. A recent assessment by Greenwell Montagu Research made the point exactly:

This plan would undoubtedly be a significant inducement to bring back funds into the country, particularly for the institutions. The prospect of a Labour election victory might even induce some repatriation to start before the election, on the following calculation. If Labour were to win and repatriation were to start on a large scale, the exchange rate would, on that ground alone, be expected to rise. In these circumstances, it might be better to anticipate that rise than be forced to buy sterling later at a higher price. No doubt there would be a lot of money going the other way, foreigners' money for example, so the net effect is by no means guaranteed. But the possibility of large scale repatriation could, for a period, hold sterling up a lot higher than might otherwise be expected. [Greenwell Montagu Research, 'The Labour Party's Emerging Economic Strategy', May 1986, p. 5].

That upward pressure will assist us in our endeavours to hold down interest rates without risking an unacceptable sterling depreciation. Its effects will be intensified in that they will influence exchange rate expectations – even in advance of the General Election. We are, I think, the first Labour Opposition which has ever been accused of first, risking the overvaluation of sterling and second, producing a rush of sterling into the United Kingdom.

Of course I am not suggesting for a moment that this one device will, in itself, be enough to secure our desired exchange rate level. Whichever way sterling moves in the short term a new Labour Government will respond with the available mechanisms and techniques open to us including, if necessary, intervention policy backed by adjustments in interest rates. And, of course, in some circumstances it would be right for the currency itself to take some of the strain. The new tax based incentive for the repatriation of overseas portfolio investments would be an added weapon in our armoury. It also has one other crucial advantage. It is a demonstration that we accept the realities of the world in which we shall become the Government of Britain and that we are already preparing to overcome some of the difficulties which previous Labour Governments did not always anticipate.

One of the more absurd claims about our proposals is that they will – in some never explained way – undermine the City's ability to attract foreign invisible trade. Our proposals will only change the balance of incentives on a small part of the City's transactions and will certainly not remove either its freedom to place investment abroad or attract foreign business.

The reason that such spurious arguments are put forward is that some in the City object to a Labour Government setting tax incentives to ensure that when the City behaves in its own interests it does not act against the interests of the economy as a whole.

Exchange rate policy is, of course, important, because of its potential effect on the rate of inflation. I do not hold the view that the inflation rate can be sacrificed for other objectives. Indeed, I do not believe that the other objectives can be achieved if inflation is allowed to get out of hand. There is agreement in the British Labour movement – the Trade Unions no less than the Party – that a sudden increase in money wages, which was produced as a misguided response to our decisions to stimulate the economy, would be bound to result in the slowing down of our employment and investment programmes. It is our clear and unequivocal view that to pursue expansion as if consequent increases in inflation were of no importance, is just as foolish as to follow the policy which has damaged the British economy over the last seven years. That policy is the apparent belief that if inflation is held down, everything else will automatically and inevitably fall into place. Experience proves that to be wrong. The control of inflation is essential. But it is only one campaign in the battle for an expanding economy.

THE EUROPEAN MONETARY SYSTEM

In the context of Labour's policy towards the exchange rate it is also necessary to address the question of entry into the EMS.

Entering the EMS as a last refuge from continual economic failure would be disastrous. It would oblige us to negotiate entry from a position of demonstrable weakness – a position from which it would be impossible for us to secure protection of our essential national interests. We should only negotiate EMS membership at a time when there is no exchange rate crisis. Negotiations could only begin when the value of the pound, whatever its level, was stable and seemed likely to remain stable.

The EMS is not a bolt-hole. Britain ought to join when – and only when – we can be certain that membership contributes to the central aims of our national policy. Even then, were we to join on the terms I set out below, the significance of EMS should not be over-stated. The fact that it is fashionable and one alternative that has not yet been tried should not make us seize membership as if our problems would all be thus solved. Membership of the exchange rate mechanism might contribute to a successful overall economic policy. But its supporters have grotesquely exaggerated the general contribution it would make to our economic welfare.

Of course, a more stable pattern of exchange rate would undoubtedly help British industry. Indeed exporters in particular say that wide exchange rate fluctuations are a major obstacle to their success. Since 1979 the cost competitiveness of British manufacture, as measured by the IMF index of competitiveness, has fluctuated by 50 per cent – more than that of any other industrialised country. That is the result of a policy which claimed as its primary aim the setting of monetary targets that would give business a stable economic environment.

What we really need is a strong economic base which will, in its turn, help to secure a strong trading performance from the British economy. That process has to be begun by a massive programme of investment in plant and machinery and skill training. Our financial policies ought to be constructed as a contribution to that end. In the pursuit of this wider policy, European co-operation can play a helpful part. But the stability of interest and exchanges rates that we seek must not be achieved at the price of sacrificing the policies which stability is intended to promote. The Labour Party is committed to investment, expansion and a reduction in unemployment. Membership of the EMS is beneficial if – and only if – it contributes to that end. That means that were we to negotiate entry – negotiating from a position of strength not from the present position of weakness which Tory policy has imposed upon us – we would insist on three pre-conditions of membership:

1. Entry at a sustainable exchange rate that both encourages United Kingdom exports and takes account of the deterioration in our balance of payments which is the inevitable result of the fall in oil revenues.
2. The co-ordination of policy which follows from a system of fixed exchange rates must be based on a mutual determination to reduce unemployment and promote expansion. That requires the stronger surplus countries to accept some of the burdens of adjustment when imbalances occur.
3. Monetary co-operation must make more use of pooled reserves and less use of competitive increases in interest rates.

To enter on any other terms would be to sacrifice our essential interests. It would also be to abdicate responsibility for the management of the British economy and to pass the decisions which affect our investment output and employment to the German Bundesbank.

Of course, the next Labour Government will want to promote and secure international economic co-operation. And as I have made clear there are circumstances in which part of that co-operation could involve the co-ordination of exchange rates. But what we need most of all – and certainly need to make exchange rate co-operation beneficial – is an international agreement to promote economic expansion. The international co-operation which we seek needs to be far wider than simple membership of an exchange rate mechanism.

7 Manufacturing Matters*

WHY MANUFACTURING MATTERS

On current trends and without governing action the UK manufacturing base will continue to contract. The West Midlands in particular will finish up bottom of every league of economic performance, whether it is measured in terms of employment, productivity, infrastructure or gross domestic produce per head of population [West Midlands CBI Survey, 1983].

These are not my words, but those contained in a West Midlands CBI survey of 70 major companies employing over 140 000 workers, published in late 1983:

Unless the climate is changed so that steps can be taken to enlarge the manufacturing base, combat import penetration and stimulate the export of manufactured goods, as oil revenues diminish the country will experience adverse effects which include:

  (i) a contraction of manufacturing to the point where the successful continuation of much of manufacturing activity is put at risk;
 (ii) an irreplaceable loss of GDP;
(iii) an adverse balance of payments of such proportions that severely deflationary measures will be needed;
 (iv) lower tax revenue for public spending on welfare, defence and other areas;
  (v) higher unemployment, with little prospect of reducing it; and
 (vi) the economy stagnating and inflation rising, driven up by a falling exchange rate.

Taken together, these constitute a grave threat to the standard of living and to the economic and political stability of the nation [*Report of House of Lords Select Committee on Overseas Trade*, Vol. 1, July 1985, p. 83].

* Based on speech to West Midlands CBI, Sutton Coldfield, 25 October 1985; speech to London Business School, 30 January 1986.

Again not my words, but those of the House of Lords Select Committee on Overseas Trade, chaired by Lord Aldington, published almost two years after the survey from the West Midlands CBI.

The Labour Party has persistently taken the Prime Minister and the Chancellor of the Exchequer to task for their neglect of British manufacturing industry. And nothing better illustrated this neglect than the response made by Leon Brittan and Nigel Lawson to the Aldington Report. More than one million words of evidence and analysis supplied by individuals, companies and trade associations representing every aspect of UK industry was dismissed by Nigel Lawson in the following terms:

> The Government therefore wholly rejects the mixture of special pleading dressed up as analysis and assertion masquerading as evidence which leads the Committee to its doom-laden conclusion.

Although the Government will not listen to industry, Labour will.

THE PARTY OF PRODUCTION

Labour is the Party of Production and after the next General Election we shall be the Government of industrial output, manufacture and visible exports. Unless we revive and rehabilitate British Industry, the only future to which our country can look forward is continuous economic decline. Not only will our national income fall further and further behind the output of our competitors. We will be increasingly unable to meet the demands of a population which sees, but cannot enjoy, the benefits which flow from a new era of scientific and technological development. Other countries will implement the improvements in medical care which we have pioneered – whilst we are unable to afford them. Other countries will improve the living standards of their people, the physical state of their environment and the systems of social security which protect their citizens against the hardships of sickness and old age. But we will find the bills beyond our means. Indeed, without a revival in industrial output and manufacture, that is the most optimistic forecast of our future. Only revival of industry can fill the gap left by the decline and eventual disappearance of income from North Sea oil.

WHAT HAPPENS WHEN OIL RUNS OUT?

For seven years we have made no attempt to prepare for the day when North Sea oil revenues run out. Instead, it has been a wasted resource – the total of the Government's revenue from North Sea oil is not even sufficient to cover the cost of the two million increase in unemployment that has occurred since the Tories came to power. There was no effort by the Conservatives to invest the proceeds from North Sea oil. Instead they have merely allowed North Sea oil exports to mask the fact that under the Conservatives manufactured trade has declined from a surplus of £4 billion in 1981 to a deficit which they forecast as £7.5 billion in 1987. This is the first time that manufactured trade has been in deficit since the industrial revolution. Oil has engendered a sense of false security in Conservative Ministers. Their complacency suggests that they simply do not understand the scale of problems facing the economy. Unless we give conscious encouragement to British industry, national income will not so much stagnate as decline.

Under the Conservatives we have lived precariously on the receipts of North Sea oil. Oil revenues account for only 6 per cent of our national income. But without them we would be bankrupt. From time to time we are given a glimpse of what life would be like when the oil revenues begin to decline. In January 1986 a reduction in oil prices demonstrated our desperate vulnerability – pound down, interest rates up, tax cuts in jeopardy. The same was true during the coal dispute, when, temporarily, we became net importers of oil again. The world recognised the fragility of our economy and the world withdrew its confidence. If we are to avoid that happening savagely and permanently as the oil revenues are continually reduced, a revival in manufacturing industry and output is essential. Only manufacturing can replace oil in our balance of payments account. But the government has written off manufacturing industry. The Chancellor, having declared himself 'at a loss to understand the selective importance attached to the manufacturing sector', has placed his hope of substantial recovery in the service sector. The Government has made a bogus comparison with America where, thanks to expansionist policies, manufacturing industry has not suffered a decline of the severity experienced in Great Britain.

CAN SERVICES FILL THE GAP?

The truth is that service industries must be encouraged to expand. But manufacturing industry remains vital to our prosperity. That is a view shared by the Director General of the CBI who, in a lengthy speech on the issue of manufacturing versus the services on 15 February 1984, stated that:

> We must avoid giving the impression that manufacturing no longer matters to Britain's wellbeing and long-term prosperity; that it can be safely consigned to the dustbin of our industrial past [CBI London Region Annual Lunch, 15 February 1984].

He then went on to criticise the Chancellor for his apparent dismissal of the manufacturing sector, and continued with the message:

> Without a buoyant manufacturing sector, the potential for growth in the service industries will be severely limited, particularly when North Sea oil runs out.

Indeed there are few people outside of the Government who believe that the balance of payments gap can be filled by the service industries providing invisible exports. It is not a question of politicians making bogus moral distinctions between the virtues and values of manufacturing on the one hand and services on the other. It is the simple and indisputable fact that services cannot fill the oil gap no matter how prosperous the City may become or what position it occupies in the international financial markets. That is the opinion even of those who work within the service industries. The Invisible Exports Council stated that they:

> do not see this growth [of invisible services] as being to a major extent a substitute for decline in general industrial activity [*Report of House of Lords Select Committee on Overseas Trade*, Vol. 1, July 1985, p. 43].

They continued that:

> it is simplistic to consider invisibles as a direct substitute for manufactured exports. Invisibles will not in themselves provide an easy answer to the run down of the manufacturing base nor resolve Britain's unemployment problem [*Report of House of Lords Select Committee on Overseas Trade*, Vol. 1, July 1985, p. 47].

Sir James Cleminson of the CBI has put the position even more bluntly:

> The growth of the service area is not only tied to its own competitiveness within the service area itself . . . but it is totally dependent on the growth of the manufacturing industry to use those services it provides [*Report of House of Lords Select Committee on Overseas Trade*, Vol. 1, July 1985, p. 42].

As the Aldington Report concludes:

> Just as much of the service industry is reliant on manufacturing, so is the export of services – like engineering consultancy, shipping, banking and insurance – heavily dependent on the export of manufactures. The majority of service industry is in any event local and non-tradeable and the idea that one can substitute for the other is misconceived [*Report of House of Lords Select Committee on Overseas Trade*, Vol. 1, July 1985, p. 47].

Only 20 per cent of service output is tradeable overseas. And far from being the phoenix that will arise out of the ashes of our manufacturing trade deficit, the UK's share of world service exports has fallen even faster than our share of world manufacturing exports. Whatever the service industries can provide, it is *not* a remedy for our future balance of payments problems.

For the service industries to progress – a state of affairs which we certainly want to see – manufacturing must march forward at something like the same pace. The success of the service industries in many of our competitor countries has been based on the understanding that it is foolish to make a choice between the two sectors of the economy.

The Government has chosen to be the champion of selected service industries. Its economic policies are clearly geared to the needs of the City, and the Chancellor himself is obviously emotionally committed to the interests of the banks, the investment institutions, the stock market, the insurance industry and the commodity exchanges. He has written manufacturing industry off and makes cavalier judgements about British manufacturing industry, which he says is not so much low-tech as no-tech, whilst the services are expected to expand to fill the vacuum that the decline in the manufacturing sector has created. It is of course a self-fulfilling prophesy. As industry is neglected –

and as exchange rate and interest policy disregards its needs –
industry contracts, whilst the service industries (some of which
benefit from the Government's cosseting) expand too slowly to fill
the gap created by manufacturing's decline. Having helped to
cause the decline and to contribute to its acceleration, the
Chancellor claims that the collapse of manufacturing industry is
inevitable and that sooner or later the economy will adjust to the
new reality. His first assertion is simply wrong. His second, if it
has any meaning at all, has a meaning which is disastrous for
Great Britain.

IS DECLINE INEVITABLE?

The dangerous nonsense about the inevitability of industrial
decline needs to be corrected. Certainly, all over the world
developed economies have experienced a *relative* industrial decline
– manufacture represents a smaller proportion of their total
output each year as increased prosperity and new technology
expands both demand and supply within the service sector. But
only in Britain has the absolute size of the manufacturing sector
been reduced. In all other major industrial countries
manufacturing has often expanded more slowly than the economy
as a whole, but manufacturing output has not fallen. In Britain
during recent years when the economy has grown manufacturing
industry has fallen in absolute terms. In America, where we are
told that prosperity depends on and is created by an expanding
service industry, one million new jobs were created in
manufacturing industry as the USARemerged from the
depression of the early 1980s. And much of the service sector
growth has been accounted for by the supply of services to
industry.

By contrast, in the UKRmanufacturing employment has fallen
by almost two million. In Britain our manufacturing base has
been eroded not by the products of South East Asia or Eastern
Europe, but by the exports of other developed countries in which
the Government encourages manufacture and the manufacturers
prosper. In 1984 all but 10 per cent of imports of manufactured
goods came from the OECDRarea and other industrialised
countries.

The need to encourage manufacturing has to be put into its

proper perspective. I do not for a moment claim that it will directly have a massive effect on the level of unemployment. Though by strengthening the economy it will enable us to pay for measures that do put Britain back to work, protect us from the balance of payments problems that expansion would otherwise create and (because much service growth is complementary) contribute to growth in the service sector itself. But what is certain is that unless we stimulate this sector of the economy the penalties will be enormous.

When asked what other way there is to protect us from the consequences of the oil revenue decline, the Government gives two answers which, whilst contradictory, are mutually vacuous. The Prime Minister says that the income from foreign investments will make up the shortfall in our national wealth. Relying on the remittance man's economy is arguably a humiliating future for the United Kingdom, but even today's much increased net flow of income from overseas does not match our declining oil surplus. These earnings, moreover, are less favourably distributed than the earnings they replace and contribute nothing to domestic employment.

The Chancellor talks of the economy 'adjusting' to the new circumstances of oil-less Britain. If that means anything outside the world of monetary mysticism in which he takes refuge from time to time, it must mean our adjusting at a lower level of output, a lower level of income and an exchange rate which has been reduced too late to encourage manufacturing investment and exports but in time to damage our standards of living.

The next Labour Government proposes to start the encouragement of manufacturing industry immediately after the Election. That means that in Government we must listen to the complaints and demands of industry. And that now – before the General Election – we must make sure that we adopt policies which create the right industrial climate. The record of the last seven years was set out by the House of Lords Select Committee:

> the paramountcy of manufacturing has not been recognised [by the Conservative Party] in the formation of policies, with the result that policies – or the avowed lack of policies – have actually been inimical to manufacturing . . . Governments of whatever political persuasion should strive for faster growth of manufacturing and in setting their macro-economic policy

should be mindful of industry's needs [*Report of House of Lords Select Committee on Overseas Trade*, Vol. 1, July 1985, pp. 60–1].

CONSULTATION WITH INDUSTRY

In laying out the macro-economic framework for industry it is far more likely that the Government will set its policy according to industry's best interests if it consults with both sides of industry. This not to say that a Labour Government will always agree with what industry says. What happens to be in the interests of one particular company is not necessarily in the interests of the UK economy as a whole, not least because the boundaries of that company may be multinational and also operating within the economic boundaries of competitor nations. Similarly, the dictates of market forces may not always work in favour of the national interest, whether because the costs borne by the nation of a company's activities are not those borne by the company itself, or because the dictates of the market's allocation of production suggest that production should take place overseas rather than in Britain. As in Japan, the government will, in the short-term, have to defy market forces to build the long-term strength necessary to be able to survive in the market.

The restructuring of the UK economy must not and cannot be left to the operation of unfettered market forces. What is needed is a new approach – economic planning. Planning for the market and planning of the market. The aims of planning are to increase efficiency and in the process take account of people's needs. Labour's planning will help British industry compete in domestic and foreign markets whilst at the same time enhancing the role of working people. Comprehensive, centralised planning is neither feasible nor desirable. It must be decentralised and democratic, recognising that it is inefficient and undesirable to attempt to plan all aspects of economic life. Planning should be selective and strategic.

Planning must be a two-way process. The Labour Government will inform both sides of industry of its priorities for industry and employment. In turn, both sides of industry will convey to Government their own demands and how they can best help the Government meet its objectives. In consultation with industry we will identify those industries, both old and new which need resources and protection to allow them to grow and mature, but which, in the longer term, can survive without constant support. We will then develop a long-term strategy for investment and growth. This will ensure that all aspects of recovery are properly co-ordinated – including training, the availability of investment finance and the deployment of technology.

No broad consensus for economic planning exists in Britain. Therefore it must be created. But it can only be created by involving people in the planning process itself. Participation is therefore essential. A step-by-step approach is required to convince people of the need for economic planning.

We intend to create a more accountable and democratic economy. Industrial change must take place through a process of negotiation and agreement. It must be part of our vision as Britain as a fairer society. Involvement and fairness are the guiding principles of our approach. Planning under Labour's new partnership with the men and women who work in our industries and services will involve consultation, co-ordination and co-operation.

It is as a forum for consultation that the Labour Party proposes to hold a National Economic Summit immediately after the next election with all sides of industry – Trade Unions, management and consumers. We need to understand industry and industry needs to understand the new Labour Government. Our relations with the Trade Unions are, of course, continual and constructive. We aim to achieve a close rapport with management to complement this.

The National Economic Summit will discuss all aspects of economic policy – priorities for public expenditure and Government intervention and regulation; taxes and incentives; improving competitiveness and efficiency; pay and other incomes; and the promotion of investment. On the basis of these discussions a National Economic Assessment will be drawn up. This will provide the framework for discussions between Government, management and Unions in specific industries, aimed at improving competitiveness and raising performance.

TRAINING

I am concerned that, despite over three million unemployed, firms are beginning to complain of skill shortages. The Labour Party takes investment in human capital as seriously as investment in physical capital. We see training as a major priority for a Labour Government. The CBI's views are important in determining the design, content and administration of our training programme.

Consultation and co-operation between the Trade Unions, firms and Government is vital if we are to tackle the drastic decline in training. Britain's post-school training is thoroughly inadequate compared with our major competitors. For every apprentice Britain trains, West Germany trains fifteen. Only a third of our workforce has qualifications, compared to three quarters in the United States. Only a fifth of young people in this country are in higher education compared with a third in Japan and over half in the USA.

Shortages of certain types of skilled labour combined with the superior training provision offered by our international competitors means that our prospects for industrial expansion have been dangerously impaired. It is vital that workers are trained for those areas of British industry that are most likely to expand in the future.

During the first two years of Government we will provide additional training places for young people and for people currently in work. Even this will only begin to restore the backlog of neglect. Trainees will have a greater incentive to join the schemes because we will increase the YTS training allowance, improve and monitor the training content of programmes and hold out the real prospect of a job at the end of each course.

The Government will expect industry to pay its fair share towards the provision of extra training – as is the case in our major overseas competitors. Whilst all firms have an interest in an increased supply of trained workers, individual firms find it cheaper to poach trained workers from other firms rather than train labour themselves. This creates a disincentive for those firms that do train. And it adds to inflationary pressures. That is why Government must step in and play a co-ordinating role in the future expansion of training.

BE PREPARED

On training and other issues serious negotiation should have already taken place. Unfortunately the CBI's 1986 Conference again demonstrated the failure of the CBI's leadership to stand up for manufacturing. Instead they preferred to attack the Labour Party.

In Australia, before the Labour Government under Bob Hawke was elected, there seemed to be an assumption amongst certain of the business organisations that, despite the deteriorating state of the economy, the right-wing Government would continue in office forever. They did not prepare properly either for the Labour Party returning to power nor the Economic Summit that followed their victory. When they attended the Economic Summit they found themselves in a weak position. They had not maintained a dialogue in the run-up to the election and because they were unprepared, found themselves unable to make a coherent impact on the proceedings.

NON-PRICE COMPETITIVENESS

The main purpose of this chapter has been to discuss the economic environment within which manufacture will prosper and expand. It has dealt only in passing with what is, fashionably, described as the 'supply-side' of the economy. The supply-side measures which we need to take – concerning the structure of the economy, its ownership and organisation – are at their most effective if implemented within the appropriate macro-economic framework. That framework must promote – not hinder – industry's progress. However, two things need to be said about the supply-side. Changes in the nature of the economy – ownership, control, concentration, location, sources of investment, the way in which decisions are taken – are fundamental to its future prosperity. Unless we change the structure of the economy we will not produce a continual long-term improvement in output and prosperity. What is more, supply-side changes are the basis of a socialist economic policy. There is no 'socialist exchange rate' – except in so much that the exchange rate which is sensible in any particular circumstance ought to be adopted by a party which prides itself on common sense. There is, however, a socialist view on economic organisation.

The changes in organisation which are set out in other chapters – new forms of autonomous social ownership [Chapter 13], new investment institutions [Chapter 10], new partnerships between workers and owners [Chapter 13] – are an essential way of helping industry to prosper. They will improve our industrial output by improving our productivity. For reducing cost – for example by a more reasonable exchange rate [see Chapter 6] – is only one way of winning new markets and expanding exports. Added value can be increased by raising our productivity, through better training, more investment and more attention to what are known as 'non-price' factors.

These embrace product design, reliability, distribution, marketing, delivery dates and after sales service, and whilst not independent of one another, or of price, together they constitute the customer's perception of the quality of the product. Design plays a key role in the whole range of non-price factors, with research and development underpinning much of it, and training as a major component.

It is hard to assess quantitatively the importance of non-price factors in trade performance, but specific industry studies and surveys confirm that in world markets the price is negotiable but the quality is not. Academic research suggests that non-price factors account for something in the range of half to three-quarters or more of the balance of customer decisions. To compete effectively, Japanese companies have relied on technological innovations and an emphasis on quality differentials, because they realise price cutting can be taken only so far if average costs are to be covered. This strategy probably explains the apparent preoccupation of Japanese management with the product itself rather than with financial management. The neglect of these supply-side considerations has led to the UK importing relatively sophisticated up-market products and exporting basic down-market goods.

This apparently simple route of improving non-price competitiveness however cannot be implemented quickly or without support from Government. It could be expensive for companies to invest in new technology, research and development. It could also be unattractive unless there is the appropriate macro-framework and a clear conception of manufacturing's role in a modern economy. Industry must take on much of the responsibility for improving performance but Government has a pivotal part to play in creating the right climate for manufacturing to adjust, expand and prosper. For six years the

Government has created quite the wrong climate for manufacturing industry. Our task will be to construct an environment in which manufacturing can flourish and grow.

8 New Technology*

THE BENEFITS OF NEW TECHNOLOGY

In the Labour Party we welcome the arrival of new technology for more positive reasons than that its domination of the economy is now inevitable. Certainly the progress of the second industrial revolution is irresistible. Industries – old and new – which do not take advantage of the benefit which new technology brings will simply find themselves out of business. And workers who attempt to hinder its progress will be trampled down by more efficient competition. But new technology is not an ogre to be propitiated by sacrifice because it cannot be resisted. It is a great force for increased wealth which – if properly harnessed – can bring Britain the growth and prosperity which has eluded us for so long.

The parallel with the first industrial revolution is important. Had we in Britain not changed the way in which we made steel, built ships, wove cloth, our manufacturing industry would not have grown and developed. We changed, and our prosperity increased. But we changed and grew more prosperous at the expense of workers who were first driven off the land and then required to pay the price of unregulated capitalism. This time, change has to be negotiated to the mutual benefit of the whole economy. Unless it is, not only will there be unnecessary hardship amongst the workers in the old industries. The actual pace of progress will be slower than would be possible as part of a co-ordinated national effort. For new technology – dependent on massive expenditure on reasearch and development as well as the training of highly skilled workers – cannot prosper within a system of dogmatic *laissez-faire*.

THE NEED FOR A STRATEGY

The rival approaches to new technology dramatically demonstrates the widening gulf between the practicality of Labour's policy and the mounting ideological hysteria of the

* Based on speech at First London Computer Week Exhibition, Earls Court, London, 5 June 1985.

Conservative approach. The Government does not appear to have a new technology strategy. Its doctrine is withdrawal from industry – all industry and every industry without examination of the individual merits of involvement in specific sectors.

Wherever the free market *may* work, it cannot work and is not working in new technology when our foreign competitors are receiving massive help from their Governments. Without such help being provided in Britain, what is already a crisis may turn into a catastrophe. The crisis is already deep – far deeper than the proponents of leaving the industry to sink or swim realise or admit. Unless changes are made quickly we may have inadvertently chosen the second of the options offered us by the Research Director of GEC – 'Either we succeed in high-tech or we become a peasant community'. The contrast between the hard practical views of such people at the sharp-end with the 'not so much low-tech, as no-tech' nonsense of the Government, could not be more stark.

In 1984, the balance of trade deficit on information technology was £2.3 billion – three times greater than official estimates and ten times greater than in 1980. The deficit is likely to grow. At an annual rate of growth of 12 per cent, Britain's information technology industry is expanding much less rapidly than are its rivals in France, Germany, Japan and the USA. Employment in the industry has fallen by 12 per cent since 1980 not risen by 4 per cent as the Government estimated. UK production has increased by 44 per cent whilst imports have risen by 110 per cent in the last five years. Unless we act quickly, another industry in which we once led the field will be dominated by our rivals – and this time it will be an industry that determines the future of our whole economy.

THE ROLE OF GOVERNMENT

The programme which the Government ought to adopt is dictated by commonsense. And so it is a tragedy of potentially immense proportions that nineteenth century ideology prevents the present Government from acting in areas where national or local government do have an essential role to play:

1. Government should supply long-term investment finance at

rates and on terms that compare with those offered abroad. And in its grants for the promotion of high technology we must get away from the 'stop–go' approach of the present Government to a policy that offers a stable pattern of assistance that properly reflects the strategic and central importance of new technology to all industries.

2. The Government must mount and fund a genuine research and development programme which relates to the real needs of all industry rather than the present undue emphasis on military projects with little civilian spin-off.

3. The Government must organise and finance the training and education of sufficient numbers of skilled and trained people to meet the needs of rapidly changing industries.

4. The Government must create an economic climate within which the changes in employment work pattern, which new technology requires, are willingly accepted by employees in the affected industries.

5. The Government must set out the above four tasks in the context of a long-term, co-ordinated plan for the promotion of new technology to ensure that essential linkages between industry's demands and the supply of research, skills, premises or finance are not lost.

The present Government has failed on every count. But in each area Labour proposes a practical and positive policy.

INVESTMENT SUPPORT

Investment is the key to increased competitiveness. It is not just the volume of investment that counts, but its type and performance. Capital productivity is as important as labour productivity and new technology offers the opportunity to improve both of these. Moreover, without new investment it is impossible to see how we can introduce new technology into existing industry or how we can help encourage the development of new high value added firms.

Companies wishing to expand into new technology or to introduce the benefits of new technology into their operations have met the problem which faces all potential industrial investors in Great Britain – the shortage of long-term funds at rates which they can afford. The problem has been particularly acute with small firms. When, in 1984, I opened the Whitechapel Computer Centre, which the Greater London Enterprise Board founded in Tower Hamlets, the companies which participated in that scheme were emphatic that if they had been forced to rely on traditional sources of finance, they would not have found the new investment which they needed. Similarly, the West Midlands Enterprise Boards have put public funds into two robotics firms along with other firms either utilising or building high technology products.

Since the INMOS investment by the Labour Government was abandoned by the present Administration, direct public investment in microchip production has been negligible.

In addition to an expanded role for Local Enterprise Boards, the main source of finance will be the National Investment Bank which will often work in conjunction with the Local Enterprise Boards. It will operate as an industrial bank along the lines of similar institutions in Japan, Germany, France, Holland and Sweden. It will lend long-term at subsidised rates of interest and back these loans with advice and a continuous close co-operation with the borrower. Priority will be given to the promotion of new technology and new ventures in both new and traditional industries – probably through a separate division of the Bank directed to this area. The aim will be to support a large number of smaller projects – often involving technology transfer – rather than concentrating on a small number of large prestige projects.

RESEARCH AND DEVELOPMENT

There are essentially four problems with research and development expenditure in this country. It is too low in absolute terms and in comparison with those countries with which we hope to compete: only two-thirds of the West German level, less than half that of the Japanese and less than one-eighth of the Americans. It has been declining and subject to uncertainty and an erratic stop–go supply of finance. It has been excessively concentrated on military projects. And finally there are insufficient links between public sector R&D and industry.

If we are to make a conscious decision to attempt a higher growth path, then we have to follow the Japanese in making a deliberate commitment to spend more on industrial R&D. Although some of this requires extra resources – both to public research bodies and in the form of grants or tax concessions to private companies – some existing resources can be released if we shift the proportion of our R&D expenditure on weapons and military projects more into line with that in our more successful overseas competitors. At present the proportion of our R&D expenditure that goes on military projects is twice that of the EEC as a whole and much higher still when compared with Japan. The chief problem with the excessive concentration on military R&D is that it both crowds out funds for industrial R&D and has very few civilian spin-offs. Moreover, it is in an area where it pales into insignificance behind the amount spent on military R&D by our chief competitors in the US and USSR military supply industries and, therefore, probably fails to give us the competitive cutting edge that the same funds applied to industry might generate. The experience with British high-technology weaponry at the time of the Falklands War leaves us in some doubt as to the effectiveness of some of these enormous R&D expenditures. And finally there is a moral dimension that some of the chief markets for military hardware are often repressive and unstable regimes. However, it is not possible immediately to switch funds from military to civilian R&D without probable adverse consequences for employment and the loss of people with research skills.

Uncertainty over the present Government's commitment to non-military R&D is having a debilitating effect. The Government has cut real expenditure by the research councils, such as the Medical Research Council. When it made substantial cuts in higher education a few years ago these were concentrated on the technological universities such as Aston, Bradford and Salford and when there were protests over Keith Joseph's student grant proposals it was the science budget that was cut instead. Then there was the Green Paper on Higher Education which proposes further closures of departments and universities including those in the science and technology fields.

The Government even imposed a five month moratorium on grants under the 'Support for Innovation' scheme. When the moratorium was lifted the Government claimed they were placing a 'new emphasis on industrial research and development'. That turned out, in practice, to amount to less support for aircraft and aero-engine R&D and less support to 'near to the market' projects on the grounds that these should be paid for out of increased private sector profitability. What all this tried to disguise was that the overall programme was cut from £308 million in 1984/5 to £295 million in 1985/6.

In addition to increasing research funding it is essential for a Labour Government to ensure two things. First, that research and development funding is put on a more stable and predictable path. Many projects take a long time to come to fruition and must not be subject to short-run vacillations in Government spending. Second, that the links between various R&D activities and industry are strengthened. Again we must follow the practical lead given by Labour local authorities. The Greater London Enterprise Board established Technology Networks centred on the London Polytechnics and University Colleges with buildings near to campuses. The aim was to get possible inventions and projects out of academe into industry. Technology Networks to harness research, development and consultancy to smaller firms are crucial because they cannot provide their own expertise in-house. The idea that has been used to justify cuts in government R&D expenditure, that increased profitability allows more in-house R&D to take place, is irrelevant to many smaller and medium-sized firms. Sometimes projects that arise from the Technology Networks can be backed by local authority money. In other cases they can be used by private industry. For example, the West Midlands County Council and other West Midlands Councils helped establish the Warwick University Science Park to house research based companies and utilise University research work. Already 19 companies covering areas such as biotechnology, robotics, information technology, computer aided design, engineering and video systems have set up there. All colleges and local authorities must be encouraged to establish science parks or technology networks in order to utilise British inventiveness because if the UK does not other countries will. Moreover, we must follow the example of France where there is now a deliberate policy of transfers and secondments between industry and research institutions.

The science parks and other local authority financed facilities are excellent examples of the way in which public sector finance – perhaps in joint venture with private institutions or our proposed NIB – can finance the establishment of adequate and suitable premises.

EDUCATION AND TRAINING

The Government's neglect of R&D is only matched by its disregard for technological and scientific education. The House of Lords Select Committee on Science and Technology described the dangers with admirable force and commendable clarity:

> If either Government or industry think that the nation's economic problems can be solved without spending money, they are deluding themselves. The nation cannot afford not to invest more.

Their January 1985 *Report* was not the only inquiry to warn the Government of the consequences of its assault on education.

Part of the problem is that for all its talk of wanting to promote science, the Government insists that this must take place within an overall decline of the Department of Education and Science budget. Quite simply it is failing to back its public sentiments with the necessary resources.

If – as we fear – the Green Paper on Education is to be implemented there is to be a further assault on higher education. Staff–student ratios are to be increased. Whole institutions are to be closed down. Others will have their research budgets cut or even lose them altogether. Cuts of such proportions will be impossible without industry feeling their adverse effects.

The UK already has a small higher education sector by international comparison. It is instructive to look at what is happening in rival countries. In Japan 36 per cent of school leavers go to university and the proportion is rising. In Taiwan the percentage is 20 per cent. Even Singapore has overtaken the UK, moving from almost zero to 10 per cent in 20 years.

Against the background of domestic cutbacks and foreign expansion the National Economic Development Office warned in 1980 that Britain was short of at least 25 000 computer specialists. Recent surveys of the Electronics Industry showed that problems of skilled labour shortage were limiting the growth of the industry. The shortages of information technology, and other suitably qualified graduates, may now be so acute that our higher education sector cannot gear up fast enough to meet the demand. The only alternative may be to send more young people to foreign universities in the interim just as some less developed countries used to send people to Britain for their training in engineering, science and technology.

As both the TUC and CBI have noted, it is not just higher education that needs a change of scale and emphasis. Education cuts have hampered the purchase of up-to-date textbooks and equipment. Skill centres, industrial training boards and apprenticeships have been decimated, whilst the effect of the Government induced recession was to squeeze firms' training budgets. Exhortations to greater efforts are no substitute for coherent and effective Government action. The CBI, for example, in *Change to Succeed* (1985), expressed their desire for:

> a partnership between the state, the education service and industry to ensure that education and training are adequate to provide business with a workforce that is properly equipped with the right skills. Education and training are likely to become a continuous process for managers, shop-floor workers and civil servants throughout their working life. Business cannot shirk its responsibility, but substantial Government involvement up to school leaving age and beyond is inevitable [CBI, *Change to Succeed*, March 1985, p. 41].

To this end, Labour is developing a co-ordinated education and training programme that recognises the need for change and adaptability throughout the system. Starting in primary schools we must get children used to handling technology, information and technological change. All children should have had some experience with computers before they leave primary school. This is probably best done by integrating the use of computers throughout the curriculum – they can be used for history or spelling as well as arithmetic and science. In the process everyone will learn to work with a keyboard and terminal.

All schools should have a core curriculum for 14–16 year olds that includes maths, science and technology. The aim is to give a more practical bias to education across the whole ability range – this is as important for the managers and graduates of tomorrow as it is for factory and office workers. And in order to ensure that we do not waste the talents of half our population, girls as well as boys will be required to do the core curriculum of science and technology subjects.

In education and training for 16–19 year olds the aim is to ensure that in addition to job specific skills, young people develop transferable skills. Youths in employment should have a statutory right to off-the-job training, whilst YTS should be substantially restructured to include a higher quality training and education component. Recent international comparisons with countries such as Germany highlight the importance of training and education in encouraging a more adaptable and efficient workforce. In order to obtain a better balance between practical and academic subjects we have to ensure that university and polytechnic entry requirements are not biased against those with more practical skills and qualifications. This will be one strand in our policy to ensure a more technologically competent workforce. But it is as important to see that people handle new technology in traditional subject areas as it is to promote technological subjects. The arts or language graduate who enters business will have as much need to be able to use new business technologies as the technology or science graduate.

THE RIGHT ECONOMIC CLIMATE

With real Government enthusiasm for advanced technology, the atmosphere in industry would be invigorated. Thanks to general Government economic policy the new technology revolution has come to British industry at a time which is wholly inimical to its willing acceptance. In fact, British workers have, in the circumstances, been remarkably agreeable to the acceptance of change – not least because many British managers have been sensible about the duty to consult and explain. If the revolution is to continue at the necessary speed, as well as improvements in investment, research and development and training, we shall need a change in the general economic climate. In fact, very little of the increases in unemployment over the past seven years has been the result of new technology. The combination of tight fiscal and monetary policies, high exchange rates and public spending cuts together with the effects of the World recession has been the real cause. Investment has been low (less than replacement in manufacturing) and much of additional unemployment is the result of non-technical causes. Indeed, in as much as some of our unemployment may be due to a relative deterioration in our competitiveness it may be the result of too little new technology not too much.

What is certain is that in the long term resistance to new technology will produce more unemployment not less. We have no choice except to accept new technology. We ought to welcome it. That requires the observance of three essential rules:

1. The maintenance of level of demand which gives workers confidence about their employment prospects in general, and the chances of successful redeployment in particular.
2. The assurance that the benefits of new productivity – the increased production and wealth – will be used for the benefit of the community as a whole.
3. Adequate consultation with affected workers about their future – within or without the company – once new technology is introduced.

New technology demonstrates the truth of the simple proposition that Britain works better when plans for economic progress are based on negotiated change and practical co-operation between industry and Government. That is what democratic socialism stands for. Our proposals for common ownership and industrial democracy are deliberately aimed at giving workers an interest and say in their industries. Workers can then influence the direction of change to ensure that it is in the interest of Britain as a whole rather than on narrow terms dictated solely by undemocratic management. Co-operation rather than confrontation seems to us to be the most sensible way to utilise the skills and ideas of workers.

A PLAN FOR NEW TECHNOLOGY

The four strands of policy discussed so far – supply of finance, research and development, education and training, and the promotion of the right economic climate – will only be really effective if they are brought together within the context of an overall co-ordinated plan or strategy for the promotion of high technology. Public sector procurement policy must be geared to the promotion of new technology particularly from UK firms in order to help build up a home base from which to launch an export drive. The US Government, for example, includes clauses in its defence supply contracts that stipulate that a certain proportion of the payment is for R&D. This is a principle that could be adopted in this country to cover non-military as well as military supplies to the public sector. Finally, given knowledge of public requirements and industrial needs, our training programme has to be geared to supply the necessary workforce.

The distinction between sunrise and sunset industries is unhelpful. All sectors should be examined to see how they can benefit from new technology. In this context labour will be trained and the NIB and the local authorities will supply the necessary finance. This cannot be a passive process – the Government waiting for approaches from industry. Government has to look to see where they can offer help to industry in a more positive way for it is precisely those staple, traditional industries that probably have most to gain from new technology that are likely to be the slowest coming forward. The scale of the problem was brought out in a Department of Trade and Industry survey:

> A quarter of managers surveyed said they had made no significant changes in their production processes in the last five years and a third said new technologies had had no impact.

> Only a fifth had any relevant professional qualification and 40 per cent of companies said they had no strategy for coping with technology at all [cited *Financial Times*, 26 March 1985].

Our training, education, research and development and finance effort can then be directed to the needs of these firms in a planned and co-ordinated way.

The Tories have become the latter-day Luddites with their emphasis on industry that is 'not so much low-tech as no-tech'. Their priority is low pay and the substitution of workers for machines. Mrs Thatcher complains of the bias in favour of machinery and so investment allowances have been phased out. Nigel Lawson expresses his disdain for manufacturing industry and so industrial and regional aid have been cut. When our rivals are increasing their Governments' resources devoted to science, R&D, and technology, our Government is cutting back. They have no vision, always looking back to the nineteenth century rather than forward to the twenty-first century.

The Labour Party is now the modern party of technology, industry and advance. It has the modern ideas and policies needed to take the out-dated and backward Britain we will inherit from the Tories into the twenty-first century. Only by anticipating and planning, investment and training, can we hope to be able to compete and pay our way as the new century unfolds. Much of what we describe is no more than obvious necessity. But obvious or not, it is not being done. Indeed the Conservatives with their bizarre attachment to the Victorian age are incapable of doing what is necessary. A Labour Government will bring simple commonsense to the development of new technology.

9 Good Government in the City*

CRISIS IN THE CITY

The City of London is facing the greatest crisis that it has faced in this century. The reason is obvious. The success of the City depends on three factors – experience, expertise and integrity. And its integrity is now in doubt. Of course, that is not to suggest that the malpractices of which we read each day are typical of all, or even most, city firms. The malpractices are, however, both numerous and growing in number. And the City itself – motivated by a misplaced loyalty to those firms which bring it into disrepute – continues to deny the need for a radical solution. Unless a thoroughgoing remedy is applied, the City itself will be the loser. In Tokyo, New York and Frankfurt they must rejoice every time a new scandal is unearthed and every time that the City responds to legitimate concern about its probity with either arrogance or complacency.

Since the City probably cannot, and certainly will not, put its own house in order, Government must provide an adequate framework for reform and an acceptable system of regulation. The present administration's reluctance to accept that obligation is the result of an increasingly close connection between the Tories and the City. The Conservative Party is now the Party of the City of London. They are bound to it with bonds just as tight as those that bind Labour to the Trade Unions. The City probably makes a larger financial contribution to the Tories than the Unions make to Labour. The City is infiltrating the Tory backbenches in the House of Commons. Much of Nigel Lawson's economic policy is directed towards the City's interests – to the detriment of manufacturing industry. The City's view of society – huge rewards for the most successful minority and the neglect of social obligation which is the product of the unregulated market – is the new Tory view of society. Cleaning up the City has become a test

* Based on Young Fabians Lecture, London, 17 December 1985.

116

of the Government's own probity – a test which, on present evidence, it seems certain to fail.

If there was ever a time when the City could be decently run like a gentleman's club, that time has passed. Because the old standards of genteel respectability are less and less fashionable among its members, the callous selfishness of Thatcherism increasingly replaces the patrician integrity of Harold Macmillan. Any system to prevent fraud and regulate conduct is automatically undermined if it is introduced and implemented by a Government which simultaneously preaches the Gospel of 'get rich quick'.

Most recent economic policy has been geared to the City's needs. Over-valued sterling, devastatingly high interest rates, the abandonment of exchange controls and the privatisation of public assets – these are the product of the Conservative/City axis. The City grows fat on the current wave of mergers and takeovers which are organised within the framework of Britain's sloppy monopolies policy. Whilst the Government takes no action to implement the tougher competition policy proposed by the last Labour Government, much of what the City does is, at best, essentially unproductive. At worst, it is positively damaging to the real economy – from which the City of London grows increasingly detached. Increasingly, instead of the City serving the whole economy, under this Government the economy is geared to serve the City. That is why concern about the City cannot be limited to a determination to end the fraudulent behaviour of a minority of its firms. We have to ensure that the City as a whole sees itself as part of the British economy and makes the maximum contribution to the whole economy's success.

Of course, the City has done well for itself during the last eight years. Pay in the City has risen much faster than in any other sector. Whilst employment in Britain has fallen since 1979 by over one million, financial sector employment has grown by over 300 000. Financial services is one of the few areas in which Britain is a world leader. We are the world's largest international banking centre and have the biggest foreign exchange market. This tradition of international business has its origins in our Imperial past – the feature of our history which for a hundred years diverted our attention from domestic investment and therefore contributed to our more recent decline. Now our position can only be maintained by allowing overseas banks and financial institutions to colonise London. In the last 20 years the number of foreign banks in London has increased almost fourfold, from 114 to 443. The likelihood of greater foreign penetration of financial services has grown following deregulation and the 'Big Bang' in 1986. The Imperial past has become a colonial present, in which we are the colony, and it is symptomatic of both the strength and weakness of that present that the City has managed to prosper while much of our non-oil economy had languished.

For no-one should make the mistake of believing that successes for the City are necessarily of benefit to the economy or the nation as a whole. The City's fortunes are not dependent upon the success of the whole economy. Indeed, sometimes, conditions which help the City hinder other industries. The encouragement of the economic environment in which the City thrives – high interest rates and an over-valued pound – has contributed to the long-term decline of the non-oil economy as a whole. The City's own profitability and expansion has been insufficient to offset the long-term decline of the rest of the non-oil economy – a decline to which it has itself partly contributed. The prevention of fraud is only one of our proper concerns about the City's future performance.

A CRIME WAVE IN THE CITY

There have been two crime waves during the past eight years. One consisted of burglaries, assaults and vandalism. The second, and bigger, crime wave, in terms of the amount of money illegally taken from its rightful owners, is taking place in the City. There was the JMB scandal in the banking sector, widespread insider dealing on the Stock Exchange, the insurance frauds at Lloyds, the Guinness affair in which the City was heavily implicated, as well as less well publicised crimes involving bogus commodity deals and phantom export credits. In the second crime wave, the criminals do not look the part. But that does not make them any less of a problem. As an *Independent* editorial said of the Guinness affair in January 1987, 'Middle class crime is always described as something else, but it is just stealing'. It went on to argue that a number of people should end up 'behind bars' for insider dealing and that it is a nonsense to call it a 'victimless crime'. It is fraud, pure and simple. It is typical of the Conservatives' double standards that their law and order rhetoric is only directed at one section of the community. In other areas the Government adopts a sterner attitude. The Government has 30 specialist Claims Control Units (made up of 175 staff) to tackle social security abuse. There are only 21 qualified investigators in the Director of Public Prosecutions' Fraud Investigation Group to tackle the far greater problem of City fraud. Of 324 serious UK frauds in 1983 only 37 led to prosecution. In the City the chances of getting caught are small, the chances of prosecution (if caught) are slim and the chances of conviction (if prosecuted) are slight. Successful prosecutions usually lead to sentences which are shorter than those imposed for similar crimes committed outside the City.

The suspicion that people are getting away with fraud in the City – at the time of writing nobody has yet been brought to trial for the Lloyds frauds – natually adds to concern about the level of fraud generally. *The Economist* claims that:

> The City of London has long been policed by bumbling inspector Clouseaus, always several steps behind those sleek pink panthers and their crafty frauds [*The Economist*, 7 December 1985].

It took the takeover of a Lloyds broker by an American firm to expose Lloyds' corruption, and a coup in Nigeria and the probings of Labour backbenchers to expose JMB and the exposure of a corrupt arbitrager by the US authorities to set off the Guinness affair. If the Government hopes to protect the City's reputation by preventing fraud from being exposed, it is not acting in the City's long-term interest. Securities, futures, options, swaps, indeed all the markets where the City shows such expertise, are increasingly dominated by large, internationally mobile, firms who could easily take their business elsewhere if they begin to doubt the probity of the City of London. Lack of supervision may help attract some trade to London from other more regulated financial centres. But it would also attract an army of undesirables who ultimately would undo the initial competitive advantage gained from a less well regulated system. In the end the reputation of the City would decline to that of a sleazy gambling house, while the honest citizens did their honest business elsewhere.

THE NEED FOR TOUGH REGULATION

We in the Labour Party take a sterner view. Our concern with fraud is not just the product of distaste or fear about the damage it is doing to the City. We believe that fraud must be stamped out if the pressures resulting from the 'Big Bang' (the end of single trading and the dismantling of commissions) are not to blow the whole City apart. This may not be a sufficient condition for City survival and success, but without a clean start the reorganisation that is to take place will face tremendous dangers. We are worried about the seemingly endless creation of new markets in new financial instruments. The end of single capacity trading and the creation of financial conglomerates will have consequences that none of us can foresee. The City needs a tough framework of statutory regulation. Without this no system of self-regulation can possibly work. The next Labour Government will provide for both.

Let me offer an illustration. The Lloyds scandals have demonstrated the inadequacy of complete self-regulation. At Lloyds – where self-regulation was carried out by insiders who were operators in the market – no one could possibly feel confident that conflicts of interest would be avoided. The regulators could only identify unacceptable behaviour by risking blemishing the reputation of Lloyds as a whole. Confidence was further damaged by the failure to prosecute known offenders and Lloyds' earlier obstruction of outside attempts to use Lloyds' documents in the pursuit of justice. The case for some sort of outside independent regulation of Lloyds is irresistible – to everyone except the Government. Lloyds has to exorcise the memory of past misdemeanours. The resignation of Ian Hay Davison, the independent Chief Executive, served to underline both fears, and confirmed Lloyds' reluctance to work outside the blinkered world of their own establishment. A large part of Hay Davison's reform package remains unfinished. The results are there for all to see, and make the case for some sort of outside independent regulation of Lloyds irresistible.

The *Financial Times'* judgement is irrefutable:

> Some of the market structures which led to past abuse are still in place and will need careful and impartial supervision: for example, there is no central auditing system for the Lloyds market . . .

So far the commercial penalties for regulatory and management failure have been few. But unless the fragile regulatory structure is partly supervised by an independent outsider there could be a recurrence of scandal in future . . .

Unless Lloyds succeeds in establishing order, the image of the whole of London's financial community could be seriously damaged [*Financial Times*, 20 November 1985].

A NEW STATUTORY FRAMEWORK

The failure of self-regulation at Lloyds has demonstrated in great detail, and with a wealth of examples of human greed, what can happen when a proud and ancient financial market subsides into the anarchy that is uncontrolled self-regulation. But it is not enough just to criticise what has happened at Lloyds however easy it is to do so. We must use this example to construct a case for a statutory framework within which subsidiary self-regulatory systems, such as Lloyds, can operate. That case has six component parts.

First the potential financial disruption is so great – and so likely to spread to other parts of the financial system with disastrous effects on confidence – that the Government has to take firm control. But as well as that overriding reason for proper supervision, firm control is also necessary:

- To deal with fraud and conflicts of interest.
- To ensure adequate prudential control.
- To ensure proper accountability for an increasingly important and powerful sector of the economy.
- To ensure that there is a tough system of consumer and investor protection.
- To improve the competitiveness of British financial institutions.

Any regulatory system must be underpinned by a coherent statutory structure. The case for statutory control is not the case against self-regulation. The two systems have to be complementary, for the services which are being regulated are constantly changing. A system which is entirely statutory may be slow to react to the pace of change in the financial services industry – and may, therefore, be more easily avoided by innovation than a system which is part self-regulating and therefore more flexible. Some practices (particularly in newly developing areas) may be entirely consistent with the letter of the law simply because legislators could not anticipate new methods of operation. But they may be outside the spirit of the law – and it will need self-regulation to deal with them. There is also a danger that an entirely statutory system becomes excessively litigious. That is certainly the case with the Securities and Exchange Commission (SEC) in the USA. We do not want a system which is slow to work and which then only provides *ex post facto* regulation rather than a more continuous supervision.

The answer is a combination of self-regulation and a statutory system which underpins it. Self-regulation is right for day to day activity – but only if it is bolstered up by a statutory framework. That means that the Securities and Investment Board (SIB) must be a statutory body financed by Government, not a private body financed and staffed by the City as the Government proposes. The SIB staff must enjoy the confidence of the City, but they must not be the City's creatures. In addition to the SIB's power to license the Stock Exchange and other Self-Regulatory Organisations (SROs) and register individuals who are entitled to do investment business, the Government proposes to use the threat of de-registration as the ultimate deterrence – a power which because of its severity will rarely be used. In addition to this ultimate and probably unusable sanction, the Labour Party proposes that the SIB should be given the power at any time to require changes in the rules of the SROs. This power will ensure a continuing monitoring of the SROs activities, prevent the development of self-protecting establishments, force them to keep pace with financial innovations and ensure that breaches of their rules are pursued both diligently and openly. As an additional safeguard we propose that the SIB should be able to initiate and bring to conclusion its own investigations and prosecutions, without relying exclusively on references from the SROs.

In short, we are not calling for the complete end of self-regulation. SROs should be made subject to much tighter scrutiny from, and accountability to, an agency responsible to Parliament. That, of course, amounts to a system of control. But we must exercise proper scrutiny over any self-regulatory system.

The precise balance between regulation and self-regulation will have to emerge from experience, and indeed may vary as new markets develop, or as the internationalisation of existing markets gathers even greater pace. There are many variations possible, but our central principle, whatever the balance, remains clear; a statutory body maintaining overall control, responsible to Parliament, and delegating powers within reasonable limits to self-regulating organisations. There is a conventional wisdom that some potentially footloose international businesses – the Eurobond markets creation in London is often quoted as an example in reverse – would desert Britain if regulation was imposed. However, a decade ago, when strict rules were introduced into the Chicago commodity markets the result (whatever the reason) was an increase in business – to the detriment of less regulated London. And in any event, lack of regulation and increase in fraud will also lead to loss of business. There is no returning to a cosier past.

Banking supervision in the wake of the JMB affair also needs a shake-up. Consideration needs to be given to the idea of a Statutory Audit Commission which could operate as an independent entity or as a branch of a statutory SIB.

The JMB scandal has highlighted the inadequacy of the Bank of England as a supervisory agency. There is a continuing danger of a conflict of interests between the Bank of England's function as supervisor and its function as central bank. The Bank should concentrate on its central banking function, passing its supervisory role to a separate body. Apologists for the present structure claim that it allows the Bank to gather intelligence as a market operator which helps supervision, and enables it to act as 'the Government's representative in the City'. There is another view which states the reverse – that in fact the Bank acts as the 'City's representative in Government'.

THE CITY'S RECORD

As the City's representative the Bank of England has supported policies which are deeply damaging to the real economy of manufacturing and output. Substantial sums of money change hands in the City. But only a small part of it contributes to new investment, provides more or cheaper finance for small firms, or helps to deal with the other long-term problems of the British economy. Money is plentiful for the purchase of existing assets as privatisation and the current merger wave demonstrates. Even in the much heralded venture capital boom much of the money is being used to purchase *existing* assets. Because companies have become more profitable but are investing less – in manufacturing below replacement levels – they have become more liquid, needing to borrow less. This has also left the banks and other City institutions looking for other lending outlets. But they have not taken a longer-run view of investment and the economy. Instead it is forcing the City's over-obsession with short-term performance onto industry, as managers in industry become more concerned with minimising the danger of short-term takeover rather than maximising long-term performance. The City, on the other hand, is keen to finance takeovers not because they are productive, but because they offer the opportunity to use excess liquidity to earn high fees at relatively low risk. More successful economies such as Japan and Germany, which take a longer run view, are not dogged by the constant threat of aggressive bids and takeovers. Many British mergers have not resulted in improved performance or higher profitability or enhanced benefits for consumers. As a result Labour's view is that each takeover bid should be much more closely scrutinised [see Chapter 11 for more detail].

Whilst in some of their specialist fields the City's record of commercial success is unquestionable, it has not enjoyed so spectacular a history of recent triumph that it can afford to brush aside all criticism. It was City institutions that bought up dud subsidiaries in America, City institutions that are still exposed to the problem of Third World debt; City institutions whose indirect overseas portfolio investments since 1979 have underperformed the world average; City institutions that finance faddish and unproductive speculations whether currently in takeovers or earlier in property speculation; City institutions that have built up overcapacity in gilts and securities that will inevitably result in crashes and failure; City institutions that have failed to provide an adequate supply of appropriate finance to industry; City institutions that have often constrained more expansionary or industry orientated economic policies; City institutions that swallowed and promoted disastrous and now discredited monetarism; City institutions that have imposed far higher administration costs on private pensions than those necessary for the State Earnings Related Pension Scheme; and it is amongst the

City institutions that we are experiencing this country's worst ever crime wave.

And when financial institutions have found that the 'market knows best' results in collapse or near bankruptcy they have expected Central Governments to bail them out – whether it is the debt crisis, regulation or secondary bank crises. It is at least, in part, fears for the consequences of Western (including many British), banks that is constraining a sensible long-term solution to the Third World Debt crisis. In the end it will probably be necessary for Western Central Governments to bail out Western banks [see also Chapter 15].

The City seems unable to recognise its own shortcomings. In the face of nearly 4 million unemployed and a net deficit of investment in manufacturing industry, they still insist that sufficient money is available for the expansion of British industry. In Germany, France and Japan the financial institutions work closely with the industries which they serve. They actively intervene to monitor and promote the companies to which they have lent in order to improve the performance of these companies. And they make long-term assessments of industrial potential. That is not to say that the problems of British industry are exclusively or mainly concerned with the supply of finance. If the City really is doing all it can then it is unclear that it should have anything to fear from new institutions such as the British Investment Bank [see Chapter 10].

Perhaps the City cannot be blamed for the fact that over two centuries there have been easier pickings in international government and trade finance. It is history that partly explains the City's orientation and comparative advantage over its international rivals. It is not to deny that the City does some things very well, to insist that some of the problems of the British economy are related to the City lack of concern for priorities other than its own!! Today the City fears a challenge to its cosy monopoly over the supply of finance, a challenge that attacks City complacency and priorities.

To leave the City to follow its own narrow interests is to neglect some of the major problems facing the British economy – 4 million unemployed, the run down of North Sea oil, and the sorry state of the non-oil, non-financial real economy. The City must be left to pursue its own affairs when they do not obstruct the overall performance of the economy – indeed it will be encouraged and facilitated in that duty. Nevertheless the contribution of the City and other service industries has to be kept in perspective. The service industries have – in Lord Weinstock's expression – to service something or someone. To some extent the City still does depend on the rest of the economy. Even those areas that do not – those areas that trade overseas – cannot fill the gap left by the rundown of manufacturing industry, as the Invisible Export Council has explained. The gap left by oil cannot just be filled by exported services. That is why the Labour Party has based the central thrust of its industrial policy on the rehabilitation of manufacturing industry.

Expectations of the City are high and in adopting a tough line we do not wish to deflect attention from other areas such as manufacturing where the problems of complacency and incompetence are often far worse. City difficulties and the problems of the non-City economy are a long way from being exclusively the City's fault. The UK banks' Third World debt problems stem as much if not more from the policies adopted by Western governments such as deflation and the decision to privatise international capital flows, the lending policies of non-UK based banks and the practices of some of the borrowers. The fears over fraud and deregulation stem as much from the slowness and inactivity of the Director of Public Prosecutions and Department of Trade and Industry. Of more than 80 cases of 'insider trading' passed to the Government by Sir Nicholas Goodison, following investigations by the Stock Exchange, only five have been brought to trial. Given that fraud and other abuses will inevitably occur amongst a small number of operators – no matter how much regulation there is – it is up to the authorities to be more active.

If we continue to run the economy mainly in the City's interest the economy will continue to deteriorate. The City will understand the Labour Party better if it understands two things. First, we will, in some areas of the economy, have different priorities and different objectives from the City. For example fat privatisation fees will stop and merger mania, with its lucrative City spin-offs, will be discouraged. Second, the next Labour Government will have been elected whereas the City will not. It will be their Party – a Conservative Government that is more closely identified with the City than any other in post-war history, that shares their values and receives their political donations –

that will have just been defeated. It will be up to the City to help put its own house in order and not to obstruct alternative economic policies. We will look to the City to co-operate and contribute. If they let the country down it will be their own fault. The onus is on them.

10 The British Investment Bank (BIB)*

THE NEED FOR THE BIB

For British companies successfully to compete in international markets, the Government of the day needs to do more than exhort them to greater effort. It is the Government's duty to create the conditions in which the competitiveness of British industry can be improved. One crucial step would be the provision of access to long-run investment funds on terms comparable with those enjoyed by their competitors in the major industrialised countries of the West. Britain, almost alone amongst the industrialised states of Europe, lacks an institution which offers substantial amounts of medium- and long-term credit – very often at preferential interest rates to special category customers. Only Investors in Industry (3is) offers anything like a comparable service, operating at only one tenth of the scale of its German or French counterpart.

To advocate such a system in Britain is to be accused of socialism. To encourage such credit institutions in Germany, Japan, France, Sweden and Holland is to be convicted only of commonsense. In France the *Crédit National* is privately owned but it works closely with the Government in providing new funds for the development of new technology, expansion of both domestic and overseas sales, encouragement of innovation and the introduction of new production processes. Its loans are subsidised by 3–5 per cent. In Germany the whole banking industry has a much closer connection with industry than is common in Britain. Amongst the German banks the *Kreditanstaldt für Wiederaufbau* (KFW) gives priority to investment in what it judges to be the overall economic interest. It provides capital to assist structural adjustment, to relieve the specific financing problems of small and medium sized firms, and to finance the export of capital goods. It also gives special priority to schemes which concern regional

---

* Based on speech at London Financial Strategy Conference, County Hall, London, 16 May 1985.

economic development and assist in preservation of the environment.

The creation of such banks in Britain will, of course, be heralded by doctrinal free market economists as wholly unnecessary. And the newspapers which support unthinking Conservatism will echo the same prejudice. But the area of industrial investment is one of the sectors of the economy where it is easiest to demonstrate that socialism makes sense. The existence of banks which understand and work with industry is taken for granted by our more successful competitors. So is the provision of low-interest loans for special categories of investment. Comparing both their credit institutions with ours and our industrial performance with theirs must convince any objective observer that we should do the same.

CHARACTERISTICS OF THE BIB

The low-interest loan will be central to the work of the BIB I want to create. But that will not be the only feature of its structure and constitution which enables it to play a significant part in the reinvigoration of British industry. The local authority enterprise boards which have saved so many companies and allowed so many more to expand, operate on commercial terms. But they have, at market rates, invested in companies which the commercial institutions have neglected. And they have done it successfully because of characteristics which they do not share with the British clearing banks, but do have in common with the industrial investment banks of Japan and Western Europe.

First, they give priority to small and medium sized companies – firms of a size which are often denied access to other sources of funds and are dependent, for good or ill, on the banks. The failure of United Kingdom institutions to meet the needs of small sized firms was identified by the Wilson Committee in 1979. An analysis of the performance of British manufacturing industry since 1979 reveals that in a majority of sectors the firms that employ less than 500 workers have recorded increases in sales, profitability and productivity which is greater than that achieved by larger companies. Yet because of the ignorance of British financial institutions they are often denied capital resources.

I say 'ignorance' because the second characteristic which sets the properly run investment bank aside from its commercial counterpart – a characteristic which it again shares with the local authority enterprise agencies – is the emphasis which it places on the need to understand industry. In Europe and Japan, the investment banks employ analysts who specialise in the organisation and potential of particular sectors. The banks become authoritative sources of judgement on the potential of a whole industry – and their investment decisions are based on more sensible criteria than just whether or not they will get their money back if the borrowing company goes bankrupt.

The case for a BIB – even one which, like the local enterprise boards, charges the market rate of interest – is very strong. But the established institutions persist with the argument that there is no shortage of funds *available* for *suitable* investment. The banks argue that the utilisation of bank facilities by industrial customers rarely exceeds 50 per cent, and that overdraft facilities are regularly renewed, so that they become the source not only of working capital but also investment funds. The problem, they say, rests with the borrower not the lender, the real rates of return on manufacturing industry are too low to finance the necessary investment. That judgement is half right. But only half right. The provision of low interest rate loans is intended to change the ratio of cost to return in such a way as to enable industry to afford the new investment. But even when that has been done there are very serious doubts about the ability of existing institutions to meet the new needs. They are *structurally* incapable of meeting all the needs of market at any level of interest rates. The increased demand that low interest investment would create would run up against the same barriers. There is only one possible conclusion to draw from the evidence of the last decade. That is that – at any interest rate – we need a new institution.

Although industry as a whole has become more dependent on bank finance, manufacturing industry has declined in importance relative to other lending – partly because of the attractions of less risky personal and mortgage finance and partly because the clearing banks remain reluctant to assist any other than the narrow financial aspects of their customers' requirements. The branch lending procedure militates against a lending manager having sufficient specialised knowledge to judge the industrial potential of a prospective investment. Even in narrow financial terms, rigorous cash flow analysis of lending propositions is not a

widely used feature. Despite the recommendations of the Wilson
Committee, the banks still pay most attention to their large
customers – companies which often have access to other sources of
finance.

The institutional case for an investment bank – close to
industry, sensitive to its needs and conversant with its problems
and prospects – is overwhelming. To keep it close to the industries
which it served that bank needs to have a regional as well as a
national structure, and to work in close partnership with regional
development agencies. The case for it providing low interest loans
to categories of industrial borrowers is equally irresistible. It is not
simply a matter of offering credit facilities equal to those which
competitor industries enjoy in Germany and Japan. It is the
essential requirement for reviving manufacturing industry. I
understand the arguments which say that the problems of many
British companies are not the problems of the size of their capital
investment, but of its utilisation. But those are arguments about
the past. For our economic future to be secure we have to increase
the *quality* of new investment. The only certain way in which that
can be done is to alter the ratio between the cost of new capital and
the return on investment. I do not minimise the importance of
increasing the return. But in the short run, that solution will not
be achieved sufficiently to overcome the timidity of the British
entrepreneur. I therefore choose a reduction in investment cost.
That choice is unavoidable to anyone who believes that Britain
cannot prosper in conditions of continuing decline in industry in
general and manufacturing industry in particular.

INDUSTRY'S PROBLEMS

The decline in competitiveness in manfuacturing industry is at the
heart of Britain's industrial decline. Central to that chronic failure
is the poor rate of performance – by international standards – of
our industrial investment.

In 1965, 34 per cent of Britain's GDP, 30 per cent of
employment and 22 per cent of investment flowed from
manufacturing industry. By 1985 manufacture's share of GDP
had fallen to 25 per cent. It accounted for 26 per cent of British
employment and 13 per cent of investment within our economy.
The pace of deterioration accelerates. For 80 per cent of the fall in

the share of employment and 64 per cent of the fall in GDP has occurred since 1973. Manufacturing employment is over 3 million below its mid-1960s peak. Real output is 6 per cent below the peak 1979 level. Net investment in manufacturing has been negative for the last five years and total manufacturing investment is 25 per cent below its 1979 level.

The fashionable excuse is that Britain's rate of decline has been matched and mirrored throughout the industrialised world as part of a natural transition to a post-industrial society. That is not so. The UK decline has been faster and has gone further than has the decline in our competition. On the most generous interpretation of the long-term figures, the proportion of imported manufactured goods which we now consume is twice as great as it was 15 years ago. All but 11 per cent of the increase comes from other developed countries, themselves 'high cost' producers. The erosion of our industrial base is more a reflection of fundamental economic weakness than that of a natural process of economic evolution.

The City of London is geared to international trade and finance. As a result, much of its success does not depend on domestic UK economic performance. Indeed, it is insulated from the domestic economy in a way that the financial institutions of most of our competitors are not – success for the City is often at the expense of the rest of the economy. The City is a highly sophisticated market for the *collection* of savings. But from the point of view of wealth creation, it is of the utmost importance that these savings should be channelled and transformed into investment in the productive sectors of the economy.

The insurance companies and pension funds only devote around 20 per cent of their money to purchasing UK company securities and much of this consists in the acquisition of existing paper rather than direct new investment. The diversion of funds by financial institutions into the financing of consumption, house price inflation, speculation, privatisation issues and capital outflows abroad has benefited the financial intermediaries, but done little for national economic growth, international competitiveness or domestic employment. In the channelling and transformation of savings into productive investment, the problem seldom lies in a shortage of potential savings or mechanisms for collection. It is related far more to the objectives and goals of the lending institutions.

FINANCE

The initial financing of the bank will come from repatriated portfolio investments held overseas by UK institutions. In Chapter 6 I outline a scheme of exchange control that will ensure a substantial inflow of funds phased over a number of years. These funds ought to be directed into the BIB in order to ensure their efficient allocation. The danger of leaving these funds to the market is that they will fail to find their way into their most productive use – instead finding their way into the speculations on property, shares and other assets. The holding of funds with the BIB by the investment institutions will attract a guaranteed rate of return in line with market returns. Risks, profits and losses on BIB loans will not determine income of investment institutions.

Although the BIB is a useful channel for repatriated funds, the case for such an institution is independent of the need to direct these funds. Indeed, in later years, as the flowback of funds from abroad slows, alternative sources of new funds will be used.

Primary legislation setting up the BIB will define the powers and duties of the Bank, the responsibilities of the Ministers to appoint its Chairman and Board of Directors, the obligations of the Bank of England to guarantee the Bank's loan stock, restrictions on the communication of commercially privileged information to Government departments and other Government agencies. The Bank will be required not to exceed the operating deficit estimated for it in the annual Public Expenditure Estimates. That deficit will, of course, be a direct charge on the Exchequer and would be reviewed each year by Parliament. It would amount to the Government's subsidy to industry and would be the only item in the bank balance sheet calculated as public expenditure. The Bank will, of course, make loans at commercial rates as well as financing low interest borrowing. The Bank itself will decide the mix between normal commercial transactions and special interest rate investment – subject only to its remaining within its stipulated operating deficit.

The Government will lay before Parliament a Statutory Instrument which sets out the criteria which guide the Bank operation. The Statutory instrument will be varied from time to time on the recommendation of the Ministers to Parliament.

LENDING POLICY

The operational guideline will lay down the practices which the
bank should observe when meeting demands for its loans. The
bank will be expected to give sympathetic consideration to
borrowing for:

(a) Projects/businesses in industrial sectors which are identified
as high growth areas.

(b) Businesses with significant export or import substitution
potential.

(c) Projects with significant regional importance.

(d) Finance research and development, innovation and
technological advance.

(e) Projects which will result in significant efficiency gains for a
particular business or industry, including refinancing or
restructuring an entire business.

(f) The costs associated with redeploying, retraining and
possibly relocating employees displaced as a result of
technological change.

(g) Projects with significant employment potential.

(h) The finance of start ups or finance for firms with no record of
innovation which wish to embark on a major programme of
new developments.

(i) Borrowing to restructure a company which has failed, or is in
danger of failing, from poor profitability, where the potential
for recovery is apparent from its assets, including goodwill,
given the use of more efficient production methods or better
management.

(j) Promote social ownership including employee buy outs.

Common features in many of these cases are that the balance
sheets of the firms concerned are insufficiently strong to raise
adequate level of debt finance from conventional sources, while
their past track records discourage subscribers of new equity.
Nevertheless, each firm offers the prospect, based on a careful
assessment of its management, markets and assets, of viability
over the longer term.

Given the gaps in the supply of finance in the UK that we have
identified most finance available from the BIB is expected to
complement existing sources of finance. There will be more
emphasis on long-term lending and a different method will be

used to assess risk. Nevertheless, I repeat that some normal commercial lending in competition with existing financial institutions is desirable:

(a) to apply further competition to those institutions
(b) to enable the BIB to be active in the market place in competition and thus keep track of market developments and indeed be at the forefront of developments
(c) to give the BIB a basis of good profitable business and indeed, as special borrowers mature and look for funding for further projects at normal rates the BIB will have the automatic means of continuing a relationship with those businesses.

In the early stages of the BIB the inflow of funds from overseas will exceed the outflow of loans. In order to utilise this surplus money it could be used to purchase Government securities, help finance our proposed public infrastructure programme and also some private infrastructure building such as combined mortgage/building finance. Some could be left to the free market to allocate.

PROJECT PLANS

In addition to the profits earned on these types of lending, loans will only be advanced to commercially viable projects. Each company receiving finance from the BIB will have to produce a project plan agreed by management, workforce and the BIB. Commercial viability will be at the forefront of each project plan proposed. The BIB will be precluded in its statute from making loans to firms that are not potentially commercially viable. The BIB will not exist to subsidise jobs or stave off inevitable collapse. It is interested in the long-term survival of firms and the development of new products, services and employment opportunities.

The project plan proposed will include information on the following:

1. Product and market strategy.
2. Location.
3. Employment levels and conditions (including equal opportunities policies).
4. Pricing policy.

5. Financial projections, including cash flow forecasts, profit and loss accounts, past and present trading accounts.
6. Future investment.
7. Technological innovations.
8. Training and retraining policy.

The project plan will have to cover the duration of the BIB loan. Since it is the intention that the BIB should develop the close working relationship with its clients that is the norm with industrial banks overseas and local enterprise boards in this country, clients will be obliged to provide periodic (say, six monthly) appraisals of the progress made under their project plans to the BIB. As the BIB will be a bank not a Government department, normal practices regarding commercial confidentiality will be followed.

Since employees as well as employers, shareholders and the BIB will all have a long-term vested interest in the success of BIB financial projects, it is essential that project plans are based on tripartite agreement. Employee participation, commitment and agreement to long-term plans will be an essential determinant of the return on, and viability of, BIB investments. Since employees are as much the assets of a firm as its fixed capital, it is sound business sense to take account of their views and ideas. Whether investment is made in co-operation or confrontation with workers is a major determinant of the cost and viability of investment. The more advanced mechanisms for employee participation and identification in many of our industrial rivals are undoubtedly other factors in their superior performance and productivity.

Close co-operation between the BIB and its client firms, along with rigorous monitoring and project appraisal are essential to ensure the commercial viability of projects but also to prevent the abuse of BIB loan facilities. The strict criteria applied to BIB loans will restrict the quantity of lending that it will be prepared to advance to industry in its early stages.

TYPES OF LENDING AND FINANCING

Depending on the circumstances and needs of borrowers, as shown in their project plan, a variety of possible types of finance could be used including:

(a) Straight lending at 'soft rates'.
(b) Lending initially at soft rates but with an interest catch up.
(c) Lending which was convertible into equity share capital.
(d) Equity share capital in the form of either preference shares or ordinary shares.
(e) Subordinated medium- or long-term loans, i.e. loans whose charge on the assets is subordinate to those of other debt holders.
(f) Participating loans, i.e. whose servicing charge consists of a fixed element plus a variable element related to profitability.
(g) Options for 'capital holidays'.
(h) Options for capitalisation of interest.
(i) Medium- or long-term loans whereby the timing of servicing and redemption varies according to the performance of the borrower, e.g. no payments in years when losses are made, up to two times annual repayment in years of profits.
(j) Project finance, provided against a variable return related to the success of the project.

Alongside small- and medium-sized firms, established multinational companies might also apply to receive BIB lending. Such lending should not be ruled out, provided such enterprises could establish that their investment projects would not attract funding from the market, though such applications would clearly have a lower priority than requests for funding from other sources.

DIFFERENCES FROM EXISTING INSTITUTIONS

Following the practice of industrial banks in our competitor economies there will be three key ways in which the terms of investment finance will differ from the type of finance generally available in the UK:

1. It will often be at government subsidised rates of interest.
2. It will be available long-term. KFW loans are generally four to ten years and Credit National loans ten to fifteen years.
3. Judgement will be made on the evidence of experts in specific industries, not on a crude accountants' calculation of whether – if the worst comes to the worst – a bankrupt firm could repay its debt.

One of the main requirements for an industrial bank is the provision to clients of expertise and advice to back up finance packages. Indeed, such expertise is necessary for the BIB to appraise the feasibility of projects, help draw up project plans and monitor and advise on progress. One of the advantages of basing the BIB on the nationalisation of an existing institution is that some expertise and structure of experience and information will be acquired. However, extensive use will have to be made of outside consultancy and secondment from industry. Detailed information on some companies and sectors should already be at hand from the DTI, the local authorities and the NEDO sector working parties. The expertise of the BIB will be one of its main distinctions from existing financial institutions. On the basis of this expertise and the more attractive terms attached to loans the BIB will be able to market aggressively the financial packages it has to offer in addition to simply waiting for firms to approach it for funds. Such marketing of industrial finance will be in line with the priorities for funding laid down for the bank by the Government in consultation with the NEDO sector working parties.

In order to allow the BIB to move into action fairly rapidly and also to help ensure a reasonable regional spread of its activities, much of its lending could be in the form of joint ventures with both public and private sector institutions, banks and agencies. These include local enterprise boards and local authority industry departments, enterprise agencies, regional development agencies such as the Scottish and Welsh Development Agencies, the National Computing Centre, the British Technology Group, the network of small business and co-op advisory and finance agencies, and possibly the nationalised industries and the MSC.

The British Investment Bank will be a centrepiece of Labour's economic and industrial policy at the next election. The most fundamental difference between Labour's policy and that of the Government concerns the production and organisation side of the economy – fashionably called the supply-side. There is a socialist supply-side. For the Conservatives supply-side policies only seem to consist of attempts to weaken the Trade Unions, juggling or rather promising to juggle taxes, transferring wealth and assets from the public to the private sector at knockdown prices, idolising the unregulated market and refusing to plan for the future. My view is that markets have to be regulated and planned and that Governments have a role in maintaining both competition and the competitiveness of firms. The Government cannot abnegate its responsibility for industry – whether private or public. In most of our more successful competitor-countries, Government is seen as having a positive role to play via institutions such as our proposed BIB. The aim of the BIB will be to make UK industry more efficient in domestic and international markets in order to secure growth and jobs for the UK.

11 The City, Takeovers and Mergers*

MERGER MANIA

The Conservatives place unqualified faith in the efficiency of the market. No Government since the war has spoken in such laudatory terms about the virtues of competition. There is much criticism of the Government for what is believed to be its encouragement of unregulated market forces. Its policy towards monopolies and mergers has usually allowed, and often encouraged, the increased concentration of British industry. Its record is deplorable.

Labour's principal objection is to the Government's willingness to see wealth and power concentrated in fewer and fewer hands. That objection is concerned both with the efficiency of the economy and the concentration of power. It is, therefore, an essentially socialist criticism. For, as Professor Alec Nove reminds us: 'the opposite to competition is not socialism, it is monopoly'. It is for that reason that monopolies and mergers policy was first introduced by a Labour Government and has been strengthened by successive Labour Administrations.

Britain is now experiencing an unprecedented increase in mergers. The 'merger mania', as it has been called, and the monopolisation of industry which it has created, demands a new and more exacting mergers policy. Yet the Government has abandoned the proposals for a tougher competition policy which it inherited from its Labour predecessors. The Labour Party will have to introduce a new mergers policy after the general election. It will form part of our plans to make the structural changes which are essential to the growth and efficiency of the British economy.

Part of that growth must come from the creation of small firms and their indigenous and endogenous growth, first to medium size and then to the status of major companies. The natural expansion of small firms ought to be a major engine of growth within the

* Based on lecture at City University, London, 23 April 1986.

economy. And a great deal of talk goes on about encouraging small firms to prosper through policies which range from a reduction in bureaucracy to their exclusion from certain items of social and industrial legislation. We too often forget that one of the things that prevents the natural growth progression of small firms is their acquisition by large conglomerates and their absorption into other companies before they have had the chance to develop themselves.

To understand the need for a new – and tougher – competition policy it is necessary to appreciate the size of the present merger boom. In 1985, the total value of mergers and takeovers was £7 billion – well over 50 per cent of the total value of all capital investment by firms. At the end of 1985, 52 per cent of the top 300 companies, with combined value of £36 billion and covering 15 per cent of the total market, were threatened by takeovers. In 1986 the total value of mergers increased to £13.5 billion, with over 1200 companies involved as pursuers or pursued in this 'merger mania'.

We should not be surprised that companies choose to shuffle their assets in this way. Domestic prospects – particularly in manufacturing industry – are so bad that there is little incentive to invest in new assets. Institutional investors are unable to resist the capital gains which flow from their involvement in takeover bids. The temptation to take the short-term view is, therefore, irresistible.

This merger mania has generated very substantial fees for the City firms which manage and promote them – many of which (coincidentally) make considerable contributions to the Conservative Party. The rush of takeovers is, in large part, responsible for the reputation of increased success that the City now enjoys – a success which is wholly unrelated to the capacity or efficiency of industry. It has also forced up share prices and thus created an illusion of real growth. Undoubtedly a number of small and select groups have benefited from the increase in mergers – merchant banks, lawyers, public relations and advertising agencies, shareholders, particularly those in companies which are taken over, newspapers (through advertising revenues) and the senior managers of the defeated companies who can expect to depart with a golden handshake. An indication of the scale of the transfer of existing wealth to the City can be gauged from recent examples. According to the *Financial Times*, had the Argyll bid for

Distillers been successful, the cost to Argyll in expenses would have been £88 million.

SHORT-TERM THINKING

The growth in asset sales does not create wealth. All it does is transfer existing wealth. The effect of these massively expensive takeovers is deeply damaging to our long-term industrial health. Not only does it result in the direction of resources into wholly unproductive purposes, it concentrates the minds of owners and managers on essentially short-term objectives – resisting takeovers, making takeover bids, maximising the advantages of being taken over. Takeovers are justified in theory by the hope that they result in the more efficient use of resources. In practice the opposite is often the case. David Walker of the Bank of England has described the growth in takeovers as creating an obsession with the short-term performance of dividends and share prices to the detriment of the long-term performance of both individual companies and the economy as a whole. Large scale investment in research and development and retaining profits or borrowing for investment – all desirable activities in themselves – are likely to hold down quoted share prices relative to the underlying asset value and make a company more vulnerable to takeover. Indeed, the absurd paradox is that companies which use available resources wisely are both more attractive to takeovers and more easily taken over than companies that simply maintain high share prices. Neither is organic growth through increased borrowing in the UK. Borrowing to expand increases a company's gearing ratio and makes it vulnerable in the present conditions of high interest rates. Growth by acquisition, often based on the issue of ordinary shares, is often the only option for expansionary companies.

The boom in takeover activity is an extension of the City's enthusiasm for short-term speculation. The motivation for takeovers is often the immediate profit which can be made during, or shortly after, the takeover, rather than the creation of more efficient firms. Indeed when there is a long-term motivation, the takeover is often carried out to avoid the necessity of improving efficiency. For the elimination of competition removes the necessity to provide a lower price or better product than other firms in the market. It is no longer simply City institutions which think of takeovers as a profit generating activity *in themselves*. Some giant companies have built up such large cash surpluses that they are beginning to assume the characteristics of financial institutions. The increased profitability of these companies should create the right environment for expansion. Using surplus funds for acquisition reduces the likelihood of profits being used for new investment. Some City firms are actually seeking out prospective takeovers, telling the putative predator of the profits that can be made and hoping to earn large fees for themselves.

Part of the pressure for takeovers is the product of the massive surplus in potential investment funds with which the City is awash. It confirms the City's long held view that there is no shortage of funds for investment. And it confirms mine that far too often the funds are not available for the right activities or at the right prices. The cash surplus stems, in part, from the decline in other markets. For example, the debt crisis has lessened the attractiveness of Third World lending. But it is also a reflection of deregulation and the opening up of the UK market to foreign funds and foreign practices. The Elders bid for Allied Lyons demonstrated that leverage buy outs – until recently an exclusively American practice – are now infecting the British market. That bid only made sense if Allied was asset stripped and broken up with the possibility that large parts of the company would pass into foreign ownership. It is probably only a matter of time before we see the first British takeover financed by 'junk bonds'.

MARKET STRUCTURE AND FIRM BEHAVIOUR

The massive changes in British market structure and balance in industrial power which are taking place in the UK, with little or no reference to the UK interest, are wholly consistent with the government's support for the free for all, as distinct from the free market. What we need now is a complete review of our attitude towards competition and takeovers.

It is, for example, possible to cite instances of where domestic competition undermines the international competitiveness of British products. In such cases we should not be constrained by a slavish commitment to the theory rather than to its outcome in practice. Similarly there are some industries – the public utilities are the obvious example – that need to be organised as national corporations. Such inevitable monopolies are best run as public monopolies and subject to stringent regulations which oblige them to pay proper regard to the interests of their consumers. The new policy must be built on the presumption that competition is to be promoted and encouraged. But its operation cannot be built on some rigid formula which automatically relates the structure, conduct and performance of a market. The degree of concentration *may* be the criterion against which the government measures the desirability of action. But it cannot be the only test. There is, of course, a particular attraction in operating a mergers policy which has the neat consistency of the formula based on concentration and market share. It protects ministers from having to make difficult decisions. But it often inhibits mergers which are necessary economically and sometimes allows mergers which are, by any standards, undesirable. One of the essential objections to takeovers – particularly the creation of larger and larger conglomerates – is that they concentrate power in too few hands. The prohibition of such a concentration of power cannot be based on any formula which simply reflects market share in one particular sector.

There are a number of reasons for this:

First, market structure is a static concept – a snap shot at a point in time. It does not take account of past or future trends and developments. In particular, it does not take account of the extent to which potential entrants into a market influence the pricing and other decisions of existing firms.

Second, there is the problem of identifying markets or spheres of rivalry between multiproduct firms.

Third, in some cases – electronics for instance – it is not always clear whether it is appropriate to think in terms of domestic markets only when much of the competition is in world markets. This was undoubtedly an issue in the Monopoly and Merger Commission's consideration of the GEC–Plessey merger proposal. Although such a merger will substantially increase concentration in the UK, the joint company would still be relatively small in world terms. However, merger is not the only option. In the car market there are a number of co-operative ventures between independent international companies such as

BL and Honda, which are preferable to the takeover of Britain's last remaining car manufacturer by Fords or GM.

Fourth, we know that in some cases it is market structure that affects a firm's conduct and performance, in others it is the firm's conduct and performance which helps determine market share and structure. An innovation may initially give a dominant position in a market to its inventor but this is due to efficiency and therefore reflects a desirable outcome. Some restriction on the erosion of market shares (via patents) may be seen as a justified premium on the return to the initial risk-taking involved in introducing an invention to the market. But excessive effort to maintain market share through restrictions on entry and restrictive practices, rather than through legitimate competitive practices of pricing and innovation, is unacceptable.

Fifth, the evidence that market structure systematically affects performance is weak.

The traditional view that industrial policy should aim to maintain competition is not enough. A policy which merely acts to maintain competitive structures (as indicated by theoretical concentration ratios) will not automatically and invariably have beneficial consequences for the conduct and performance of individual concerns. Yet it is upon that naive view that the Government has based its policy towards the non-privatised sector. It was the principle upon which Norman Tebbit, then Secretary of State for Industry, based his 1984 statement on competition policy. And more recently, Sir Gordon Borrie, the Director General of Fair Trading, has welcomed that statement as clarifying the criteria by which we decide on a merger reference to the Monoplies and Mergers Commission. Whilst the Director General's support for clearly definable terms of reference is understandable enough, the revision in competition policy should not primarily be concerned with making life easier for senior public servants. Naturally enough industry welcomed the new predictability that the Tebbit guidelines provided. But it has simply served to increase the confidence of bidders and promote merger activity. Indeed one of the reasons why the pre-1984 policy was to be preferred to what has followed it was that it contained an element of discretion for the Director General, and Commission judgements had to be made about public interest as well as levels of concentration.

THE NEED FOR A NEW POLICY

The record of mergers during the last seven years is not one which justifies a relaxation of policy. A London Business School survey showed that in half of the mergers which they examined the shareholders in the acquiring firm would have been better off if the merger had not taken place. Evidence from the Liesner Committee (set up by the Labour government in 1978) and later confirmed by American experience, suggests that most mergers do not produce the increase in profits and efficiency their proponents promised.

The motivation for a high proportion of all mergers is an increase in monopoly power and a reduction in competition. Yet only 3 per cent of mergers are referred for investigation. Given the poor record of many mergers and the undesirable side effects of merger activity, the discouragement provided by the more pragmatic approach which preceded the 1984 declaration acted as a desirable disincentive. Before 1984, the presumption on which an investigation was carried out, was that – in the absence of proof to the contrary – the merger was desirable. Any company which, in those circumstances, lacked the confidence to risk an investigation was clearly short of rational justification for its merger proposal. The classic excuse concerned the time taken for the Commission to report. And clearly in some cases it operated far too slowly. Mergers intended to produce an improvement in performance should maintain their attraction even after an investigation lasting for a few months. There is a case, however, for speeding up the procedure for investigation by adopting some of the provisions of the Hart–Scott–Rodino legislation in the USA. This would give the Office of Fair Trading and the Merger Panel 30 days to decide whether to recommend a reference or not.

In short, there are three main reasons why a tougher mergers and monopolies policy is necessary:

1. The classic objection to market concentration – the abuse of monopoly power, diseconomies of scale and the costs of integrating two companies.
2. The record of mergers over the recent past which demonstrates that, at best, they have had a neutral effect on growth and efficiency.
3. The increasing emphasis – in the City and some major

companies – on merger activity rather than real growth with the consequent shortening of time horizons which diverts managerial resources and acts to the detriment of new investment and research and development.

NEW RULES

But, of course, that does not justify a general prohibition of mergers. We have to devise a system which prohibits those which are undesirable, and allows those which are beneficial to proceed. It is not – and never can be – possible to set our criteria against which every merger can be judged or every merger reference determined. Some rules can easily be promulgated.

– Mergers above a specified threshold must be pre-notified to the OFT. At the same time the employees in the affected companies must be warned of the proposals and given an opportunity to represent their views to the OFT.
– The burden of proof must be changed. Liesner recommended a neutral stance – a movement from the assumption of desirability to agnosticism. We now need to go further. The policy must be based on the premise that, unless proved otherwise, the merger is undesirable.
– When a merger is approved, a reporting procedure must be introduced which shows whether or not the objective of the merger – which may have appeared both desirable and attractive at the time of the application – has been achieved in practice. If these reports show that the merger has failed it must be possible to impose sanctions against the company such as the prohibition of price increases or price roll back – unless the failure can be satisfactorily explained or rectified.
– The power to break up undesirable monopolies should be maintained. It will be used rarely. So it is far better to prevent than to remedy. As Professor Kenneth George, a part-time member of the MMC has put it:
  since merger policy involves making judgments about an uncertain future, errors of judgment are bound to be made, and some areas are more easily corrected than others. If, for instance, the mistake takes the form of preventing the takeover of a company which subsequently performs badly

there are self-correcting mechanisms at hand in the form of a loss of market share and for exposure to a further bid. However, if the error is to allow a merger which, with hindsight, should have been stopped, the corrective mechanisms such as de-merger or effective control of the monopoly are less certain to come into operation [K. George, *Fiscal Studies*, Vol. 6, February 1985, p. 47].

These policies will – in themselves – reduce the number of merger proposals. And that will, in itself, be a beneficial result. But other deterrents to undesirable mergers are necessary. Three trip wires should trigger pre-notification of merger proposals to the OFT:

1. The size of mergers that (automatically) qualify for pre-notification should be £15 million. The government should make clear that it proposes to discourage small firms from being absorbed by large competitors rather than expanding naturally.
2. The national and regional market share criteria should be reduced from the current level of 25 per cent.
3. Bids should be *automatically* pre-notified when the foreign stake exceeds 15 per cent as is the case in Australia.
   (It is worth noting that with the increased internationalisation of the security market there are days when more shares in some UK companies are traded in New York than in London. It is at least worth examining the advantages of requiring bids for UK companies to be made in UK security markets.)

In addition to those takeovers referred to the MMC by the OFT, three further trip wires will trigger automatic investigation by the MMC.

1. Bids which involve defence or strategic interests where – in the opinion of the Monopolies and Mergers Commission – the merger may be in conflict with the public interest in general.
2. All acquisitions of national and regional newspapers.
3. Mergers constructed in ways which clearly make them purely financial transactions rather than commercial or industrial transactions (i.e., the implication is that assets would have to be stripped out to repay the borrowing incurred for the transaction).

It must be recognised, however, that with present policy the problem is not only the detail of existing legislation, it is the lack of use of powers already in existence that accounts for the very low numbers of referrals and the failure of existing policy to contain undesirable mergers and merger activity. Until there is time to legislate the Labour Party will operate existing criteria much more tightly.

At present, unless there is a reference to the MMC, there is no obligation to consult employees about matters which may have important implications for their jobs, employment conditions and pensions. We would make it obligatory for bidders to declare details of the effect of their plans on the future size and shape of the workforce, at the time they are pre-notified to the OFT. As with other undertakings made at the time of a merger, these could be subject to recall and examination following the merger. We could usefully learn from the Netherlands whose merger code provides for employees to be informed:

– Of merger talks at an early stage.
– Of the reasons for a merger.
– Of likely social, economic and legal consequences.
– Of measures designed to alleviate their effects.

Such a package of rights for employees at the time of takeover or merger bids could be incorporated in wider legislation designed to encourage employee participation and give employees more rights to information and consultation.

Britain has one of the world's most concentrated economies. And we have an economy which grows increasingly inefficient, with decision-making dominated by financial rather than economic considerations. It is therefore in the interests of the consumer and our society in general that far more genuine competitiveness be introduced and, where necessary, imposed. Otherwise, companies and financial institutions, if left to their own devices, will continue to act in restraint of competition. The Tory Government talks of the need for competitiveness but, in practice, it bows to the will of the City and positively encourages the market to be uncompetitive. It is our view that the City's interest in making a 'fast buck' on a merger is rarely in the interest of the nation as a whole. And it is in stark contrast to its relative lack of concern for the real economy. The Labour Party believes in controlling monopolies and mergers in pursuit of economic efficiency and consumer choice. We intend to act accordingly.

12 Pension Funds and the Public Good*

THE PUBLIC GOOD

It is difficult to imagine a more intellectually inadequate assertion than that by which the CBI and National Association of Pension Funds attempts to set out the principles on which pension funds should operate:

> Pension funds should have one duty only – to their pensioners. They should not be obliged to concern themselves with any outside interest, even the public good.

The error inherent in that *obiter dictum* is that the welfare of the pensioner and the public good are, or may be, in conflict with each other. That is clearly absurd. Even if the only duty of pension funds is to maximise the return to their members – a concept which is arguable but is at least not meaningless – what is loosely described as 'the public good' is directly related to that objective. For the income which pensioners receive comes from a variety of sources. The ability of some of the funds to sustain continually high levels of payment will be determined by the 'public good' – if, not unreasonably, we include within that definition the strength of the economy.

Future pensioners depend for their income on four types of provision – the basic state pension, state earnings related pension schemes, occupational schemes and private savings and pensions. Each one of those sources is dependent on the performance of the national economy because this affects the growth of earnings of contributors, the growth of earnings of pension funds and it even affects the dependency ratio – the comparison between dependant pensioners and employed workers. If we do not regard pensions as 'positional goods' – that is to say receipts which are important not because of their absolute value but because of the way in which they distinguish the recipient from other people – the private

---

* Based on speech at Pension and Investment Resource Centre Launch Conference, London, 3 November 1986.

150

pension fund, no less than any other form of provision, has the strongest vested interest in the success of the whole economy and should construct its policies accordingly.

This is not to suggest that there are not other factors which influence the level of pension receipts – for example, the performance of individual pension fund managers, the level of overseas investment and the tax and legal framework. The point is that a large number of factors are crucial to the pensions level. Let me take the obvious example. All the evidence suggests that – apart from the occasions when it provided an opportunity to speculate in sterling – overseas investment of pension funds receipts has not produced an appreciably higher return than domestic investment. But even had that not been the case, a substantial outflow of investment would not have been to the advantage of the pension fund recipients themselves – even if it had improved their short-term return. For the result would have been an effect on the British economy which reduced their pension income from domestic sources.

The adverse effect of such foreign investment is psychological as well as directly economic. I quote from John Plender:

> The greatest worry in the wake of the abolition of exchange controls is that fund managers have been given an open invitation to indulge the same profound pessimism about British economic prospects that afflicts so many in the upper elements of government and industry . . . And at what point does this apparent pessimism about Britain's economic prospects become self-fulfilling? [J. Plender, *That's The Way The Money Goes*, André Deutch, London, 1982, p. 196].

A second problem flows from pension fund managers believing, and being encouraged to believe, that they live in a world of their own. Despite the essential long-term interest of pension funds, the performance of their managers is often judged in terms of short-term results – switching investment between sectors or climbing on the back of the inflation in equity prices during a takeover bid. That is certainly not the way to maximise the performance of the whole economy. It may not even be the best way to maximise the long-term income to the fund.

The Chancellor of the Exchequer, having encouraged a short-term perspective by his privatisation programme, his support for unregulated market forces and the consequent fluctuation in exchange and interest rates, is now a belated convert to the longer-term view. David Walker, Executive Director of the Bank of England, has listed the problems that flow from the short-term investment perspective that is produced by 'merger mania'. He suggests that the institutions should hypothicate part of their funds for long-term investment. Of course, if all funds followed such advice, it would avoid any of them being (in the short term) at a competitive disadvantage.

THE GOVERNMENT'S DUTY TO INFLUENCE BEHAVIOUR

The truth is that under the present regime, the pension funds are probably doing neither what is best for the British economy or for their future or present pension recipients. Ironically, the managers enjoy constant congratulation – and their increasing esteem is reflected in constantly increasing salaries. Here is not the place to digress into the fascinating psychological, philosophical and indeed sociological questions concerning whether or not we should *expect* pension fund managers to behave differently. Whilst they are able to set both their own targets and their own rewards it is unlikely that they will change their habits. However, the Government has a duty to influence their behaviour. Pension funds own, in aggregate, £200 billion of assets. That includes 30 per cent of all shares traded on the stock exchange. Power of that magnitude is too great to ignore.

Previous chapters [Ch. 11 and Ch. 6] have already advanced policies which will reduce short-term speculative activity and encourage pension funds to invest in Britain. They set out how we will operate a more rigorous scrutiny of takeovers and mergers and how we will introduce a system of fiscal benefits and matching penalties which will act as an incentive to concentrate institutional investment within the UK.

Our plans for a tougher policy on mergers and takeovers will help to discourage the current obsession with takeover bids. Pension funds often have a central role in these battles which, whilst often producing an inflation in paper values do not usually produce a matching growth in real output or real values. Too much concentration on takeovers tends to cause an obsession with short-term thinking by industrial managers to the detriment of the real economy. This is despite the fact that the long-term nature of pension fund liabilities ought to enable pension fund managers to take a longer-term perspective.

THE RECORD OF PENSION FUNDS

It is perhaps important that we keep the myth of the omnipotence of the professional manager in some sort of perspective. Over the last seven years the average UK equity fund has achieved a lower return than the UK stock market average, as measured by the FT All Share Index – lower by 1 per cent a year. Although disparaging remarks are often addressed to socially responsible investment (SRI), by contrast the Friends Provident Trust, which bases its portfolio on a list of socially acceptable companies, out-performed the FT All Share Index by 8 per cent in the two years since its launch. A report by the Council on Economic Priorities on two large Californian public pension funds whose assets totalled $17 billion in 1980, found that when two areas of investment in companies with corporate investments in South Africa and poor employee relations were excluded, it did not have any significant financial consequences for the fund's performance. Foreign investment in equities and bonds by UK pension funds – an area which has seen substantial growth from 9.9 per cent of new investment in 1978 to 27 per cent in 1985 – has also produced a poor performance. According to the survey by Wood Mackenzie (covering 66 per cent of pension funds) between 1980–85 following the lifting of exchange controls in October 1979, the average sterling return on UK investment was 26 per cent, the average sterling return on overseas investments was 24.2 per cent, whilst the MSCI World Index showed an average sterling return of 25.8 per cent – significantly better than investment overseas by UK pension funds but worse than their return on their investments in the UK.

Not surprisingly the Pension and Investment Resource Centre (PIRC) has noted a growing view in favour of passive fund management in which 'a fund invests in all (or most) of the companies in a particular stock market index'. According to the *Financial Times* (2 July 1986), there is 'growing evidence that . . . the average pension fund consistently achieved substantially lower returns than the stock market index'. The *FT*'s conclusion is categoric. 'A six-year-old child, even a chimpanzee, will, on average, do just as well as the professionals by picking a portfolio of shares at random.'

Perhaps because funds still prefer to employ highly paid managers rather than children or chimpanzees, there is a danger that what we observe is increased turnover and trading, rather than increased performance. In 1985 the equity portfolios of pension funds were twice as active as in 1978. This trend is likely to continue following the 'Big Bang' much to the delight of dealers in the City who make money out of continued trade and movement in prices rather than out of the underlying performance of the assets they sell.

Sometimes investment managers have claimed to me that their poor performance both relative to the UK and relative to the rest of the world stock markets has been offset by currency gains. In other words they have said that they have used British people's funds, subsidised by the British taxpayer, to speculate against sterling and the British Government. Such speculative movements as well as being disliked by UK industry may also have contributed to high real interest rates.

Certainly the repatriation of some UK funds across the exchanges and the associated disincentive to managed funds to invest more than a certain proportion of funds abroad, will enable us to achieve a lower rate of interest than would be the case without such a scheme.

NEED FOR ACCOUNTABILITY AND REGULATION

Whatever the reasons given for the less than spectacular performance of the professionals there is a strong case for them to be subject to tighter regulation and accountability so that they are under obligation to justify their investment decisions. Frequently the professionals make investments on the grounds that 'they know best' without ever having to justify their assertion. Too often fashion rather than objective criteria determines the choice of investment. There is a suspicion that their definition of what they professionally judge to be in the best interests of the funds they manage is what they happen to be wanting to do at any moment in time. Too often personal enthusiasm or individual prejudices are regarded as more important than what is good for the UK or even what is good for their pension fund. For instance freedom to choose foreign investment is not an object in itself. But it has become elevated into a moral principle. The prejudices include the assertion of pension funds' rights to act in secret. If pension fund managers are as good as they say they are then they will welcome the recommendations of the Wilson Committee for greater disclosure of information and increased accountability to the people whose deferred pay they are managing. They should welcome the chance to prove to a wider audience how responsibly they have invested other people's money. They will be glad to have the opportunity to show that they have considered all domestic UK returns and opportunities for diversification before investing in higher returns or more satisfactory diversifications overseas. They will also be able to justify their views on the political donations to the Conservative Party made by the companies in which they invest on the grounds of the Conservative Party's contribution to success in sectors such as manufacturing and construction! And finally they will want to explain why they did not use their substantial shareholdings in companies to influence and monitor the decisions taken by the managers of the companies they own.

The important point is that there is clearly no one correct or objective view of the appropriate levels and types of different investment to be carried out by pension funds. Personal judgement and opinion do come into the decision. That is the only possible explanation for the wide differences in the overseas holdings of different pension funds. Indeed, some pension fund managers may have difficulty in providing a rationale for selecting one level of overseas investment rather than another. Often they are dependent on local advisers for advice about foreign investment rather than their own in-house research. Yet John Plender has suggested that:

> There are signs . . . that some pension funds feel instinctively happier taking big risks overseas than small risks at home [J. Plender, *That's The Way The Money Goes*, André Deutch, London, 1982, p. 195].

AN ALTERNATIVE APPROACH

The fact that existing arrangements are far from perfect should lead us to ask whether there is scope for alternative investment strategies for pension funds. Local authority pension funds, partly under the auspices of information supplied by the PIRC, are beginning to lead the way. There are many unexplored areas for local authority pension funds within the bands of existing legislation. The Queen's Counsel opinion obtained by Southwark Council in 1985 would seem to suggest that local authorities may be at fault if they delegate investment decisions to outside pension fund managers. This would give locally elected councillors, who in turn can consult with representatives of pensioners and employees, the opportunity to develop alternative investment strategies to those served up by their City managers. This does not remove their obligation to take appropriate outside advice nor to try to achieve reasonable returns or an adequate diversification of assets. But since as we have seen, choices in investment decisions do arise between different investment options with adequate returns, then they can give more scope to carry out targeted or socially responsible investment. This may involve taking a longer-run view which is appropriate given the longer-run nature of their liabilities. It may involve targeting more investment in the local or UK economy. It may involve not investing in South Africa or companies with South African connections. These are options which can be explored and which under existing legislation and existing evidence of relative returns should be explored.

Socially responsible investment is not an alternative to financially sound investment – indeed its return looked at over a longer time horizon may well be better than conventional investment strategies. SRI is probably legitimate even within existing legislation because obligations to acquire an adequate rate of return on investments does not specify a time period. If SRI yields equal or superior returns to conventional investment, there should be no problem and this obviously applies to the bulk of SRI. A pensions lawyer, John Quarrell, has commented that:

> If trustees can fulfil financial criteria and at the same time fulfil moral and social views while investing then the courts will protect them. There is no duty in law to invest overseas or in what might be considered, in some quarters, socially or morally unacceptable areas, but they must at least consider them, and if after due consideration they feel that they can invest the monies under their control as well as if not better than if they did invest

in these areas, then they are protected [Speech to National Association of Pension Funds Conference, 5 May 1984].

However, because there may be some controversy or debate over the returns to SRI local authorities are quite sensibly only gradually building up the SRI component of their portfolio. Southwark, for example, is setting aside just 10 per cent of their investment for long-run, targeted or socially responsible investment. A number of London authorities and other public pension funds have invested a small amount of money in the West Midlands Regional Unit Trust managed jointly by the West Midlands Enterprise Board and Lazards. In London 13 borough pension funds are linking up with Guiness Mahon to set up a London Development Capital Fund. Nottinghamshire have invested pension fund money in local property. All of the SRI initiatives I have described only apply to a proportion of diversified pension fund portfolios whilst other parts of the portfolio are managed along more familiar lines.

Over the next few years, as local authorities come to realise and develop the positive use of their pension funds, the legal position should become clearer. If a Labour government finds that further legislation is required then they should legislate to clarify the position of trustees.

The idea that further legislation or restrictions in this area would be controversial should seem bizarre to those with overseas experience. Many states in the USA place restrictions on the amount of funds that can be invested in certain categories of shares and some also insist that a certain proportion of funds be invested locally in categories such as housing. Canada restricts overseas investment to 10 per cent. Overall, the US legal position seems to be appreciably more relaxed than ours. For example, in 1978, a new supplement to Scott's *Law of Trusts*, one of the standard statements of American trust law, advocated reliance on moral and social considerations in fiduciary investments:

> Trustees in deciding whether to invest in, or to retain, the securities of a corporation may properly consider the social performance of the corporation. They may decline to invest in, or to retain, the securities of corporations whose activities or some of them are contrary to fundamental and generally accepted ethical principles. They may consider such matters as pollution, race discrimination, fair employment and consumer

responsibility [cited Michael T. Leibig, 'The Case For Alternative Investments', *Studies in Pension Fund Investments*, vol. 3, Union Printers, 1980, p. 12].

We need to consider whether there is a case to bring UK legislation more into line with that existing in the USA.

Some try to present socially responsible investment as financially unsound investment. That is not the case. Financially unsound investments by trustees would be socially irresponsible. The choice of investments that pension funds should make is between socially responsibly financially sound investments on the one hand and socially irresponsible investment whether financially sound or unsound, on the other hand.

There must be more effort to ensure that trustees or their advisers have to account for the social effects of their investments and provide information as to whether they are considered more socially responsible alternatives. This move needs to be backed by legislation to implement the proposals along the lines set out in the Wilson Report including the proposition that boards of trustees have at least 50 per cent representation from the potential or actual beneficiaries of pension funds. Legislation in this area must be backed by the new rules for takeovers and mergers, the change in the tax regime for institutions overseas investment and the establishment of the NIB that have been set out in an earlier chapter [Chapter 10]. In addition legislation will be needed to end sex discrimination in superannuation schemes and, if necessary, to clarify the position of the obligations of local authority pension funds.

13 Social Ownership and Industrial Democracy*

NOT JUST NATIONALISATION

In examining the use for public ownership the discussion ought not to be about the need to extend the public sector but about the method by which the extension is made.

Labour's previous arguments on the subject have been prejudiced by failures of both language and logic. The linguistic complication concerns the word 'nationalisation', a term sometimes used to describe social ownership in general and sometimes employed to define one particular form of public enterprise – the state monopoly owned by the Government and managed by a board of ministerial nominees.

In the public mind the two definitions have become confused. Social ownership – indeed Socialism itself – has become identified with the remote and bureaucratic state corporation. In fact the commitment in Clause 4 of the Labour Party constitution 'to secure for the workers by hand and by brain the full fruits of their labour' can be fulfilled in a number of ways. It may mean a state corporation that provides national ownership of a public utility. It may mean a single publicly owned company created to compete with private sector rivals. It may mean worker or consumer co-operatives, which are not the property of the general public at all. All these forms of organisation are embraced by the title social ownership. The founding father of the Labour Party never intended that we should commit ourselves solely to what has come to be called 'nationalisation'. Sydney Webb who wrote the constitution which includes Clause 4 Part IV was absolutely specific about what that commitment meant:

> This declaration of the Labour Party leaves it open to choose from time to time whatever forms of common ownership – from co-operative store to the nationalised railway – and whatever form of popular administration and control of industry – from

* Based on speech at *Socialist Economic Review*.

159

national guilds to ministries of employment and municipal management – may *in particular cases* be appropriate [B. Webb, *The Diaries, 1924–43*, Vol. 4, Virago, London, 1985].

It was Webb who emphasised 'in particular cases'. The author of our constitution was committed to a flexibility which has not always been evident in the arguments of some advocates of public ownership. We have to realise that if we are committed to a more equal distribution of power as well as of wealth, the old Morrisonian model does not meet our needs. The miners do not feel that they have much control over the working of the Coal Board. The John Lewis Partnership is commonly assumed to be in the private sector. But the man or woman who works in one of its stores has a greater influence over the conditions of work than any miner could realistically claim.

In this chapter I argue for an increase in social ownership. But I do not propose an extension of nationalisation. If all we espoused was the creation of more Government monopolies some of our opponents' criticisms might be justified. A society in which a higher percentage of productive capacity is owned by the state is unlikely to be highly efficient or truly free. Social ownership should give power to the people not to the Government. It is meant to diffuse wealth and influence, not concentrate them in the hands of Ministers and civil servants.

State monopolies are sometimes justified as instruments of national planning. But in practice what that amounts to is often 'rationalisation' and 'elimination of surplus capacity' – or in plainer language, closures and redundancies. The fulfilment of the real planning function is best typified by the results of the 1948 Transport Act which undertook to create 'an integrated transport system'. Thirty years later the integrated transport system is no nearer. But we have closed a large number of railway lines.

The problems assume an extra dimension when social ownership is extended to manufacturing industry. The management of public utilities at least partly accepts that they were created to behave in a way which distinguishes them from the private gas works and the London Midland and Scottish Railway. On the other hand, British Steel and the Coal Board seem desperately anxious to behave as if they were privately owned.

Of course, some of the problems of the nationalised industries are less inherent within their structure than imposed upon them by the Government. The NCB did not have to be run by an elderly American who rejected workers' involvement in management with the zeal of a nineteenth century plantation owner. Nor did the Government have to set external financing targets for the gas and the electricity industries which increase prices, hold down wages and produce an artificially high profit which is syphoned off and used as a surreptitious indirect tax. But some forms of social ownership would make such direct Government intervention impossible. If social ownership is to meet the needs of the 1980s and 1990s we must create new forms of enterprise which exist independent of Government.

Nationalisation – monopolies owned by the state and insulated from detailed, parliamentary control – remains the right model for the public utilities. Basis industries, on which the whole economy depends, ought to remain under the control of Central Government. That is why we propose to return British Gas and British Telecom to the public sector. Strategically sensitive industries, like oil and airlines, should also have within them a nationally controlled company. But that is not an argument against different forms of organisation in different sorts of enterprise.

SOCIAL OWNERSHIP AND ECONOMIC EFFICIENCY

We seek to extend social ownership into manufacturing industry with the insistence that each new enterprise must operate with competitive efficiency. We cannot afford, politically or economically, to use the public sector as the casualty clearing station of the free enterprise battle ground. Whoever was responsible for attempting to prop-up the night storage heater and soft drink co-operative set back the cause of social ownership by years. The general rule must be that public firms contribute to the efficiency of the economy. That does not prevent them from being good employers.

In R. H. Tawney's words:

Whether in any particular instant social ownership is desirable or not is a question to be decided in the light not of a resounding affirmative of the virtues of either free enterprise or socialism, but on the facts of the case [*Acquisitive Society*, Wheatsheaf, Sussex, 1982].

The facts of the case today call for a substantial extension of social ownership though not of centralised state monopolies.

The object of that extension is threefold:

(a) To improve the efficiency of British industry by creating the opportunities for and availability of the new investment which private institutional sources have failed to provide

(b) to improve price competition by setting the pace in industries which were previously dominated by monopolies and oligopolies

(c) to involve in the management of businesses of all kinds, the men and women who work within them, thus:

– defusing power and influence
– promoting a commitment to success of the enterprise
– tapping enthusiasm and skills which are too often wasted.

The achievement of these aims is as important to the consumer as it is to the worker in the socially owned industry. It is monopolies – private and public – which have held prices artificially high and depressed the quality of the product. A commitment to success includes and involves pride in the product which the enterprise is producing.

We dismiss the objective of tapping enthusiasm and skills as intangible or sentimental at our peril. The world's most successful economies – in societies as diverse as Sweden and Japan – have built on the understanding that the worker has a stake in the firm's success. Yet in Britain we allow our industry largely to be owned by absentee landlords – pension funds, life assurance companies, unit trusts and multinational corporations which are as remote from their employees as nineteenth century landlords. Our future depends on British workers believing that British industry belongs to them. That belief can be most easily and honestly encouraged by extensions of autonomous social ownership.

A PLURALITY OF FORMS OF SOCIAL OWNERSHIP

There is no universal blueprint for every sector or industry. So what we need now is:

(a) Single companies, initially owned by the state but rapidly turned into common property by extensions of industrial democracy.

(b) Companies owned or sponsored by local authorities.

(c) Consumer and worker co-operatives.

(d) More public investment in private companies bringing with it influence which equity capital ought to copy.

Two further forms of social ownership deserve special consideration:

(a) The single socially owned company, competing with the private corporations which make up oligopolies and thus contributing to a more rigorous competition policy. Britain needs tougher monopolies and mergers legislation. But one way of reducing the concentration of power is to take over or set up socially owned counter weights – in banking, sugar refining, the provision of concrete and construction material and construction itself. And since the Government is determined to privatise the airlines and oil industries, a substantial public presence must be recreated there. Such new or reformed companies will have to involve the work force in their management. Otherwise they may revert to the old pattern of 'nationalised industry', indistinguishable from private companies.

(b) The local authority sponsored company may sometimes be a wholly owned enterprise which is the natural horizontal extension of a service which the council provides. But most local authority industrial involvement will be concerned with a type of activity described in simple and stark terms in a brochure distributed by the West Midlands Enterprise Board: 'We invest at fully commercial but very competitive terms. No subsidies or grants are given . . . Control of a company remains and will continue to remain with the shareholders.' As an assertion of rampant ideology that statement leaves something to be desired. But all over Britain it is being applied in a way which fills a vacuum left by the timid and unimaginative investment institutions.

SWEDISH EMPLOYEE INVESTMENT FUNDS

A new scheme for providing workers with real economic power

and meeting the needs of an expanding economy is now being introduced in Sweden. It is worth our sympathetic consideration for it is intended to increase public ownership in a way which improves national economic performance. The scheme proposes that a special profit tax and a pay roll levy be allocated to an investment fund which is run by five regional boards on which workers have a majority of members. The object is to obtain co-operation in creating a high profit economy in which the profits are reinvested.

History shows that high profits do not, in themselves, automatically generate beneficial investment. And it also demonstrates that Trade Unions, whose co-operation is necessary for a successful incomes policy, are reluctant to take part in such an essential operation when profits rise abnormally high – even if there is a statutory control on dividends. For a wage increase, once foregone, is never regained. But a retained profit adds to the value of the asset. To ask Trade Unions to contribute to a high profit economy requires us to promise both the reinvestment of those profits and a Trade Union voice in how the reinvestment is distributed.

Such a scheme can contribute to a major shift in economic power, for, over the years, the new investment funds, largely controlled by representatives of the workers will make up a gradually increasing share of each company's equity capital. The scheme assists in the re-distribution of wealth as well as of power. And it makes more risk capital available. In short, it is exactly the sort of scheme that we should be examining in the Labour Party – looking for ways of making corporate wealth more associated with the workers in individual companies and less the property of giant national or regional institutions.

EMPLOYEE SHARE OWNERSHIP

Another way of providing employees in both public and private industry with a stake in their companies is to enable them to hold shares which carry the same rights to participate in choosing management as are enjoyed by other shareholders. The extension of employee shareholding if it carries with it the rights which part ownership is supposed to convey) is wholly consistent with the aims of socialism – the more equal distribution of power and wealth and the consequent emancipation of working people. It is also in the interests of the economic success and social cohesion of this country. But those benefits will only result from the extension of genuine schemes for employee participation which carry with them influence as well as dividends. Cosmetic schemes, which are not available to all employees, which amount to no more than executive bonus payments, which are intended to reduce rather than extend the influence of individual employees over the conduct of their companies and which are treated as cheap alternatives to wage increases, will not do. Genuine share incentive schemes increase the wealth and influence of the employees who take part in them, as well as contributing to the economic performance of the companies. The Institute of Personnel Management cite the following evidence from the USA:

> when ownership is spread widely through a firm, the company is likely to be more successful than a similar business without employee ownership. On the other hand, if an ownership scheme is confined to managers, this is usually counterproductive. The resentment of the other employees is likely to make the firm less successful in spite of the additional motivation given to managers [IPM, *Practical Participation and Involvement, Vol. 5, Pay and Benefits*, 1982, p. 72a].

There is thus a considerable overlap between progressive industrial relations practice and the promotion of employee ownership.

According to the CBI: 'about one in three companies have either profit sharing or share ownership schemes, roughly double the number five years ago. Half of these schemes extend right down to the shop floor'. The next Labour Government ought to encourage the extension of such schemes – providing that they fulfil the requirements which I have described. The obvious way to promote them is through tax policy.

The 1978 Finance Act profit sharing scheme should be extended by the removal of the legal limit on the extent to which shares can be made available.

Employee buy outs should be encouraged by removing present loan and tax disincentives, provided that the equity is reasonably shared amongst all employees. Measures to help this process include:

(i) The extension of interest rate relief for purchases of shares by employees to a period much longer than the present twelve months.

(ii) Applying the same incentives to employees who want to buy shares subsequent to the initial share purchases as those which applied at the time of the initial purchase.

(iii) Applying the interest reliefs to trusts purchasing blocks of shares collectively on behalf of employees.

EMPLOYEE STOCK OWNERSHIP PLANS (ESOPs)

One of the chief problems in extending employee share ownership is the criteria laid down by the investment protection committees of the big institutional investors such as insurance companies and pension funds. Their fear is that, notwithstanding the evidence of improved performance when employees are given a stake in their company, the value of their shareholdings will become diluted as new shares are issued to employees. They, therefore, stipulate that firms in which they invest should not allocate more than 5 per cent of their pre-tax profits or 1 per cent of their existing share issue to employee shareholders. To meet this problem we ought to look at the establishment of trusts which can purchase *existing* shares on behalf of employees without diluting the value of other shares that remain. Unless this is done the investment protection committees will put a brake on employee shareholding which tax incentives will not be able to overcome.

It is also important to relate the tax incentives to the retention of the share by the employees of the firm in which they are purchased. The tax exemptions should positively encourage retention as well as be lost after premature resale. In other ways the rights carried by the employees' shares would not be fundamentally different from those enjoyed by any other shareholder. I do not want the acquisition of shares to result in the day to day detailed management of the firm. I want the employees to own it – retaining the last resort powers which are proper to ownership and which influence the general strategy of a company simply by their existence. But to fulfil the socialist objectives of wider employee share ownership we will need more than tax incentives. We will need the structures – the institutions – which give reality to the theoretical powers of share ownership. One practical lesson can be learned from the United States of America where Employee Stock Ownership Plans (ESOPs) are being established at a rapid rate. These involve the creation of a trust which borrows money and uses it to buy shares in a specific company. The Americans have encouraged the creation of ESOPs with a series of tax breaks. These include concessions on loans, employer payments and sales of shares to ESOPs and on dividends accruing to ESOPs.

These tax measures have been buttressed by loans from Government agencies to ESOPs, the establishment of ESOPs within public sector companies and the insistence that ESOPs be established as a condition of Government aid to some private sector companies such as Chrysler. In America, according to *International Business Week*, 7000 companies operate employee shares in the company which employs them. Indeed America, the home of free enterprise, is second only to Sweden, the paragon of democratic socialism, in the speed at which it is increasing employee shareholdings.

In the UK the Labour movement is not waiting for the next Labour Government to examine the feasibility of ESOPs in this country. Within the bounds of existing legislation, Unity Trust, the new Trade Union financial institution, is carrying out research in collaboration with City experts into new ways in which employees can be given a stake in the businesses for which they work. The hope is that the British will be able to learn from American experience in order to create British ESOPs that fit our own legal and social environment.

Whilst there have been success stories amongst the American ESOPs, there have also been a number of abuses which we must be careful to avoid. First, in some cases the benefits from the ESOPs have been unfairly distributed around the workforce with management receiving a higher share of the proceeds than their warrants. Second, the shares in ESOPs have often not had voting rights with the result that whilst ownership resides with employees control does not. Third, employee pension funds have sometimes been used to set up the ESOPs. This is undesirable as it is better that pensions are based on a broader range of assets than just those of the company in which the employee works. In attempting to adopt some of the pioneering ideas of the Americans to this country it will be necessary to take account of their experience in order to avoid the shortcomings of some of the American schemes.

One way that an ESOP could become established in this country is for each year the company involved to pay a profit related bonus to the trust. That payment would be eligible for tax relief. The received profits would gradually repay the initial loan and free some of the shares for distribution to employees. These shares would – under the terms of the 1978 Act – be free of income tax as long as they were held for five years by employees of the company. Employees would thus acquire rights in the future profits of the concern in which they work. The company itself would both qualify for tax benefits and, in many cases, tap additional investment resources without selling out to a conglomerate or allowing ownership to pass to the institutions. Most important of all, the economy would benefit from the increased emotional involvement of employees in the company which now employs them and which, in the future, they would partly own. That benefit can flow from many different forms of participation.

EMPLOYEE PARTICIPATION

As well as the extensions of share ownership and co-operative enterprise, the pluralistic mixed economy which I want to see will also involve a substantial extension of what is popularly called employee participation – the formal involvement of representatives of employees within the decision-making structures of the companies which employ them.

Although good employer practices are being introduced in some progressive firms it will require legislation to hasten their widespread adoption. Employees must be given a legal right to information and to be consulted. The Labour Party therefore favours some of the EEC Directives in this area – in particular the Vredling Directive and the 5th Directive. Indeed, the legitimate criticism of these directives is that they do not go far enough.

Unless employee share ownership schemes are coupled with rights to information, consultation and representation they may be treated with justified suspicion by many Trade Unionists. Giving more say to employees will not come for a long time – if ever in some large and multinational companies – if we just rely on ownership schemes. Ownership schemes must therefore be accompanied by other measures if they are to have a really beneficial impact on employees and industrial performance.

A combination of all these forms of greater participation is likely to increase commitment and reduce the great psychological barrier to change and innovation in British industry – the employees' feeling of alienation which is far more pronounced in our immobile and unequal society than it is in the economies of most of our competitors.

A recent study of West German industry demonstrates the undeniable connection between participation in decision-making and productivity – an absolute increase in productivity per worker of 15 per cent resulted from the introduction of greater participation. And the American Centre for Employee Ownership concluded from its study of 360 high technology companies that those which shared ownership with most or all of its employees grew between twice and four times as fast as companies in which the employees owned no stock.

CHANGING THE MIX OF THE MIXED ECONOMY

I am for the diffusion of wealth and power – in principle. And I rejoice that the methods of bringing such a diffusion about are likely to improve our economic performance. The creation of co-operatives and the acquisition, by employees, of shares in the companies which employ them – coupled with rights to promote employee participation – is a far more effective way of providing economic enfranchisement than the creation of vast state monopolies which are often insensitive to the needs both of workers and consumers and, under the present government, exploit their monopoly powers in order to make a contribution from their profits to finance tax cuts.

The time has gone for us to assault the sector of private ownership in a head on charge. Rather should we penetrate the whole system, thinking of the mixture of the mixed economy not as two separate and incompatible sectors with an impregnable boundary line which sometimes changes its position, but as two economic systems which can overlap and mutually benefit each other. I therefore advocate extensions in co-operative enterprise, employee shareholdings and employee rights to information and consultation as the way in which socialists should seek, in modern conditions, to extend the boundaries of social ownership. They are, in fact, one of the most practical ways by which social ownership can be extended. Critics would be right to argue that some schemes are undesirable. But whilst on occasions the practice is imperfect we should not turn against the principle.

TRADE UNIONS AND EMPLOYEE OWNERSHIP

We should not believe that Trade Unionism will be undermined. Trade Unions exist to enhance the power and the prosperity of their members and most of them will want to encourage schemes which have that effect. What is of more immediate importance, the introduction of employee ownership schemes could actually enhance Trade Union influence. It will often be Trade Unions which propose the adoption of, let us say, employee share ownership as, in the past, they have proposed the adoption of pension plans, redundancy agreements and sickness benefits. It will often be the Trade Unions which make sure that share ownership schemes are available to the whole workforce rather than simply to executive and management grades. The involvement of employees in the ownership of their companies solves a second dilemma which has, for all this century, complicated the Trade Union attitude towards industrial success. It concerns profits. The market system has given profits a bad name. They are too often looked upon as what makes dividends not what finances new investment and new jobs – and often that judgement is justified. Certainly it is unreasonable to expect Unions to co-operate in the sensible division of national income if they know that the money earnings which they forgo are automatically transferred into profits which may be used for purposes which are inconsistent with the interests of their members. Employee ownership requires Trade Unions to take a positive interest in the whole operation of the companies within which they organise.

CO-OPERATIVES

Of course, the most effective form of employee ownership is the co-operative – the company which is not only completely owned by the employees who work for it but which is organised in a way which enhances their general control over strategy and distributes that eventual power equally amongst all the partners. For co-operatives, the evidence of the extra strength created as the result of worker participation is overwhelming – much of it provided from abroad since Britain lags behind other industrialised countries in the creation of co-operative enterprise.

Nevertheless the number of UK worker co-operatives has trebled in recent years and now about 200 new co-operatives are registering per year. The survival record of these new co-operatives is far superior to that of new private companies of similar size. Moreover, where Labour local authorities have helped to establish co-operatives the cost of the jobs generated has only been about £3000 per job, much cheaper than for other schemes such as Enterprise Zones.

Part of the failure to increase co-operative organisation even more rapidly lies in the British tax system which discriminates against co-operatives. Many incentives available to private companies are denied co-operatives:

– The business expansion scheme cannot apply to co-operatives since the share capital they possess belongs to the workers within the company.
– Losses made by *individuals* on share holdings cannot be written off against tax in the case of co-operatives because there is no ordinary share capital.
– Schemes which allow retained earnings to be shared amongst workers by the issue of share options cannot apply to co-operatives because of the need of its share capital to be redeemable when a worker leaves employment.

The next Labour Government must find ways of overcoming these specific disadvantages. Indeed it must find a method by which the encouragement of genuine co-operatives is specifically encouraged. I define genuine co-operatives as concerns which are owned by the workers within them and in which:

– Each worker holds a share of equal weight to every other share and it is relinquished on retirement.
– The return on external capital invested in the co-operative is

limited to what amounts to interest for the external funds supplied.
- The value of the business is inherited by future generations of workers or the community at large.

Two sets of tax measures could be introduced to promote co-operatives:

(a) Measures to encourage conversions of existing private companies to co-operatives:

 (i) Elimination of capital gains, clawbacks of capital allowances and succession of losses where an existing company is converted into a co-operative.
 (ii) Elimination of capital gains and capital transfer tax liabilities that would normally accrue when a business changes hands.

(b) Measures to aid the supply of finance for co-operatives:

 (i) Restoration of a lower rate of corporation tax for co-operatives. This is the norm in many other countries and also applied in this country until 1984 when the Conservatives abolished the lower rate for co-operatives.
 (ii) Ensure that the tax reliefs contained in the 1978 and subsequent Finance Acts that are available on employee shareholding, profit sharing and stock options are paralleled by an equivalent tax regime for co-operatives.
 (iii) Profits allocated to a co-operative's statutory indivisible reserve to be free of corporation tax. This would increase the funds available for investment. The members of the co-operative would not be entitled to the assets of this reserve if the co-operative closed down.
 (iv) Tax relief on loans by co-operative employees to their co-operative.

Since these represent considerable incentives to co-operatives it is essential that the definition of who is eligible is tightly defined. The danger, otherwise, is that firms will temporarily convert to co-operative status to take advantage of the tax concessions before converting back to private status at a later date. Another possible problem is that the build up of the capital value of co-operatives may encourage members to liquidate and take the capital gain. Both these problems can be averted if only firms with a statutory indivisible reserve warrant co-operative status and the tax concessions. If the co-operative closes down the reserve can be allocated to co-operative agencies to help finance other co-operatives.

AUTONOMOUS SOCIAL OWNERSHIP

The creation of autonomous socially owned companies will provide for our economy the stimulus which it has traditionally lacked – the feeling amongst working men and women that they have a vested interest in the success of the economy.

I therefore argue that extensions of employee share ownership – like the creation of worker co-operatives – are likely to improve our economic performance. But I advocate them as having virtues in themselves – irrespective of the undoubted material benefits that they bring. Those benefits should not surprise us. John Stuart Mill – regarded by many people who have either never read or failed to understand him as one of the New Liberalism's major prophets – argued that the control of an enterprise was best left in the hands of those who have the strongest vested interests in the concern's success. Those people are not, as is often mistakenly supposed, the shareholders. They are the workers whose whole livelihood depends on the performance of the company by which they are employed. In case you suspect that I am misinterpreting one of Mill's most famous aphorisms, let me quote to you from his *Principles of Political Economy*:

> the form of association however, which if mankind continues to improve must be expected in the end to predominate, is not that which can exist between a capitalist as chief and workpeople without a voice in the management but the association of labourers themselves on terms of equality: collectively owning the capital with which they carry on their operation and working under managers elected and rewarded by themselves [J. S. Mill, *Principles Of Political Economy*, Vol. 3, Longman, London, 1871, p. 352].

The creation of autonomous socially owned companies will not absolve the Government from direct intervention in the economy. Firm competition, prices and location policies will still be needed to ensure that every form of independent enterprise observes national as well as sectoral interests. But we must abandon the idea of a mixed economy in which the public and private sectors are wholly distinct from each other. There are common characteristics in both privately and socially owned companies. The time has come to blur the distinction between the two systems. As well as occupying more of the private sector we need to penetrate the whole capitalist economy.

We ought to advocate that course of action for reasons which are largely unconcerned with ideology. Of course, the creation of a more equal society is an article of faith. And a radical change in the pattern of ownership is essential to the achievement of that ideal. But supporters of public ownership are no less economically hardheaded than supporters of private enterprise.

The case for participation combines moral imperative and practical necessity. But we should not just think of it purely in terms of the practical benefits it provides.

R. H. Tawney wrote that:

> it is idle for a nation to blazon Liberty, Equality and Fraternity, or other resounding affirmations on the facades of its public buildings, if to display the same motto on its factories and mines would arouse only the cynical laughter that greets a reminder of idealism turned sour and hopes unfulfilled [Tawney, *The Radical Tradition*, Allen & Unwin, London, 1966, p. 147].

Removing the cynicism which affects much of our industrial organisation will improve both our economic performance and the whole quality of our national life.

14 Pay Cuts, Profit Sharing and a National Minimum Wage*

OLD THEORIES IN NEW BOTTLES

The Chancellor of the Exchequer continues resolutely to march backwards into our economic past – confirming the old Keynesian doctrine that plain men, who claim to eschew theory and concentrate on practice, usually do no more than apply the theories of a bygone age. Mr Lawson – retaining as Chancellor the habits he picked up when a journalist – is always particularly excited by old ideas that have been dressed up to look as if they are new. The latest is profit sharing – an idea currently popularised by Professor Martin Weitzman, taken up by the SDP because they find the latest fads irresistible and now adopted by the Government as a headline catching alternative to introducing the changes in policy which the economy so desperately needs.

The idea was to offer tax concessions to workers who first take a cut in basic pay, as a result contribute to increased company profits and then receive a share of the profits which is more or less equivalent to the basic pay cut. The proposal is, in truth, less 'profit sharing' than 'wage sharing'. For the absolute concession comes from the workers. During a recession the shareholders would still benefit from the wage cut. But wage earners would not receive their share of profits. Of course, at the introduction of a profit sharing scheme tax concessions associated with its introduction could make workers better off. But the tax concessions would be temporary. That alone should make Union negotiators ponder before they mortgage their members' future. The superficial attraction of the temporary tax cut of up to £5 per week suggested by the Treasury in order to get their profit sharing scheme off the ground should not be underestimated. But there is no doubt that there are better uses to which the money could be

---

* Based on speech to Monday Business Luncheon Club, London, 2 June 1986; speech at Fabian Society Conference, London, 27 November 1986.

175

directed – a lower tax rate band or the encouragement of more genuine forms of employee ownership. Alternatively the money spent on the proposed tax cut would create more jobs if spent directly on capital investment and maintenance.

Two claims are made for profit sharing. The first is that it will more closely identify workers with the interests of companies which employ them. I am wholly in favour of that aim. That is why we have advocated an extension of employee share ownership plans, and the introduction of genuine and comprehensive industrial democracy. But I cannot believe that profit sharing will achieve that desirable objective of ending the detachment and alienation which characterises too much of British industry.

PRACTICAL PROBLEMS WITH PROFIT SHARING

Profit sharing would mean that weekly pay packets and monthly pay cheques would vary with a company's performance. But most of the decisions which determine performance and therefore pay would be taken by managements which the employees neither controlled nor influenced. If workers are to share in the entrepreneurial risks inherent in market-led private enterprise, then they will quite rightly expect to have a substantial input to vital strategic decisions on investment and production. Shareholders do not expect to shoulder financial risk without representation and neither do employees. Moreover, it is easier for the shareholders to sell their stake if they are unhappy with their returns than it is for an employee to leave the company.

The Lawson proposals start from a much narrower perspective – to increase the flexibility of employee remuneration, but on the employer's terms only. The impotence, as well as the precariousness, of the workers' position would increase their alienation. A worker told that pay had been cut because the Board of Directors had made an unwise investment or because commodity prices had risen is not likely to feel an increasing commitment to the company. The idea that the worker and company will thrive if the workers' pay is related to profits is based on one of profit sharing's underlying – and offensive – fallacies: the notion that failure to make adequate profits is usually the responsibility of the worker and, in consequence, workers can keep pay and profits high by working harder.

Employee alienation is also likely to be increased by the inevitable wrangle about the extent and level of the profits which are to be shared. The record of corporation tax returns shows us that many companies invest considerable effort in 'profit avoidance'. Many of Britain's most profitable companies have not paid corporation tax for years. The hostility of the CBI and British management to even modest proposals for extending consultation and providing information – Vredling and the EEC 5th Directive – does not increase confidence that British management would be open and honest about its real profits. The TUC has pointed out further practical problems. The bargaining units for pay negotiations are rarely identical with the profit centres in companies or indeed the reporting unit for Stock Exchange purposes. Although public companies are under legal obligation to publish profit and loss accounts, there is no legal requirement to identify the profit centres where surpluses are generated. Clearly a workable system of profit sharing is dependent on an extension of the legal framework covering financial information. A scheme which proposes profit sharing which neither describes how profits are to be defined nor requires them to be disclosed is not to be taken seriously.

Indeed it is difficult to believe that the Chancellor has considered any of the practical consequences of his proposal – other than the divertionary headlines which it produced on the day after his lack-lustre 1986 budget. Does he, for example, expect Britain's 8 million low paid workers to participate? For they can barely live on what they receive now and certainly could not afford variable wage levels which sometimes vary downwards. If they are not included, how would more highly paid workers, in companies which employed men and women on low pay, be able to participate? And what effects would variable pay levels have, even on the lives of the better paid? Would building societies calculate mortgage entitlement on basic wage alone or on basic wage and an estimate of possible profit share? The Chancellor's plan ought not to be confused with other schemes – the John Lewis Partnership, for example – in which wages are negotiated against normal criteria and profit bonuses are then paid in addition to established rates of pay. Real profit sharing is far too close to socialism for the Chancellor's taste.

DO PAY CUTS CREATE JOBS?

One argument offered in support of profit sharing is the claim that they will increase – or at least reduce reductions in – employment. Clearly that argument was particularly appealing to the Chancellor. For since he is not – and within the terms of his present policy cannot be – making any real attempt to reduce unemployment, any gimmick that creates the illusion of action is to be welcomed. Equally clearly, profit sharing, as proposed, will not reduce unemployment by any significant figure.

Whilst some people certainly regard profit sharing as a back door method of imposing pay cuts, others argue that the wage cuts involved would be only temporary but the flexibility it created would, they say, have a permanent effect on employment. In his budget speech Nigel Lawson appeared to employ both these arguments talking in terms of wage flexibility and pricing people into jobs.

Advocates of wage cuts have three circumstances in mind in which employment is helped. The first is where lower wages improve international competitiveness. The second is where cheaper labour means that more labour intensive technologies of production are used because wages are lower. The third is where lower wage costs are passed on to lower prices leading to an upturn in demand and production.

In the real world there are problems with all these assumptions which undermine confidence in the academic profit sharing proposals on which Lawson bases his argument.

Despite its appalling unemployment record the UK is by no means a high wage country. We also know that low wages are no guarantee of a job for it is the low paid who are most likely to become unemployed. That should not surprise us. Low wages and managerial incompetence often go together. The UK has completely failed to make significant inroads into the higher wage, more research intensive manufacturing industries of the future. Low wages may help compensate for low investment and lack of innovation, but they can only delay the need for structural adjustment of the economy, not remove it. We are not losing markets to Germany, America and Japan because of relative wage levels. They pay higher wages, but they also invest more. And if we fight for world trade by starting a crazy wage-cutting competition, it is South East Asia which will always win.

In practice many of the technologies that firms invest in do not lend themselves to a simple switch to more labour intensive forms of production and then back again to higher levels of technology when conditions change. Wage cuts designed to make manual labour more competitive against machinery are just a modern form of Luddism. Anything designed to slow down the march of technology – including the Prime Minister's promise to 'end the tax bias in favour of machinery' – will only make Britain less competitive in the long run as compared with countries which have welcomed and encouraged progress. We ought not to complain about the machines, but make sure that their product is properly distributed. All that is likely to happen with pay cuts is that certain people would still lose their jobs but those left in the firm would suffer a loss of income as well. And we cannot automatically expect that wage cuts will get passed on to price cuts. The reason that many firms cut output and jobs rather than prices has nothing to do with wage rigidity. Firms can often see no advantage in cutting prices – especially if they suspect that their rivals can easily follow them with price cuts of their own. In many markets all firms have an interest in keeping prices high and then each firm competes for market share through innovation, advertising and marketing. A classic example of such practice is the UK car market in which prices are much higher than overseas but none of the major companies can see any point in cutting their prices whether their cars are produced in high wage or low wage countries. It is inconceivable that Ford or General Motors or BL would change their pricing policy in response to the Lawson proposals for profit sharing.

A further difficulty with generalised wage flexibility is that at a time of recession, a fall in wages will only serve to reinforce the downturn in demand. Falling real wages in the early 1980s undoubtedly had this effect.

WHY DO FIRMS NOT CUT WAGES?

If firms really believe that what they wanted was more workers at lower pay why is it that at present with 3½ million unemployed, firms still prefer to raise real wages rather than employment?

It is not just in response to Trade Union pressure for it also happens in non-unionised companies. It is a deliberate act of policy by managers who see pay as a means of retaining and motivating employees. Pay is not a cost that is crudely minimised in the way the textbooks would have us believe. Indeed, many firms will raise wages rather than employment because they believe that this is most consistent with profit maximisation. Whatever the reason – and the habit is common amongst members of the CBI Council even though they advocate wage restraint for others – it is not clear what difference profit sharing will make to this phenomenon. Indeed as firms have emerged from the depths of the recession they have preferred to rebuild profit margins rather than output and employment. Things would have been no more than marginally different under wage flexibility.

LABOUR'S ATTITUDE TO PROFIT SHARING

The arguments in favour of profit sharing based on motivating employees are much stronger than the grandiloquent and exaggerated claims about its rejuvenating effect on employment. The question is whether profit sharing is the best means to achieve improved employee motivation and identification.

Labour's attitude to profit sharing can be easily summarised.

We believe that it is a legitimate area for collective bargaining along with pay, fringe benefits, health and safety and so on. To say the least we are sceptical about its so-called job generating potential. At best the effect is likely to be marginal and therefore it is not a substitute or an excuse for a proper jobs programme as the Government seems to hope. The question therefore arises as to whether it is worth spending the large sums on it envisaged by the Government. If the aim is jobs then the money could be better spent – on hospitals, education, capital projects or reducing employers national insurance contributions.

If the aim is to encourage employee identification and involvement this can best be achieved through extensions of employee ownership or co-operatives [see Chapter 13].

THE EXTENT AND COSTS OF WORKING POVERTY

In putting forward proposals for variable wages, even for those on

low pay, the Chancellor has shown that he does not understand
the full extent of working poverty in Britain. Working poverty is
increasing in Great Britain:

- 8 000 000 British workers, of whom 6 000 000 are women, earn
  wages which are less than two thirds of average male earnings –
  £115 a week or its part time equivalent.
- 680 000 workers have incomes of less than the supplementary
  benefit level.
- 4 110 000 workers have incomes which are less than 140 per
  cent of supplementary benefit level.

Those are Government figures. They are an extraordinary
indictment of our divided society.

The defence of below subsistence wages is based on the
assertion that the economy can afford nothing better. That
assertion is based on a total misunderstanding of the costs to the
economy which low pay imposes. The truth is that society is
subsidising employers who pay low wages. I give two examples:

- 1.3 million recipients of housing benefit are in work. The cost of
  their benefit to the Exchequer is £500 million.
- 200 000 households (containing 500 000 children) have their
  wages topped up by Family Income Supplement. The total cost
  to the Exchequer is £100 million.

In addition to the direct, and easily calculable, costs, there are the
costs which we too often ignore because they cannot be identified
in Government statistics – the extra costs, for example, which are
imposed on the health service. The correlation between low
income and poor health is absolute and irrefutable.

Of course, the major burden of low pay is not carried by the
Exchequer but by the low paid themselves – calculated in terms of
poor diet, bad housing, inadequate clothing and reduced
prospects. When we talk about the *cost* of a national minimum
wage we too often forget that it is not so much an addition as a
transfer. Low paid workers – in catering, distribution, clothing
manufacture – are subsidising (through their inadequate
standard of living) the purchasing power of the better off.

The introduction of a national minimum wage is essentially an
exercise in redistribution. It will, in my view, eventually produce a
more healthy and more dynamic economy. But it has to begin as
part of a concerted national effort to aim the distribution of

resources towards the lowest paid. That is why the TUC and Labour Party document *Low Pay: Policies and Priorities* [July 1986] insists that the implementation of a national minimum wage must be discussed – and the details decided – as part of the National Economic Assessment. In that forum, representatives of the TUC and industry will join with the Government in considering the annual allocation of resources. Clearly the speed and level at which a national minimum wage can be introduced must be discussed there in the light of prevailing economic circumstances. But we will not discuss it oppressed by the propaganda that a national minimum wage will imperil the success of the economy. A recent OECD report on the French economy concluded that the introduction of a minimum wage had no significant effect on either wage inflation or employment.

THE TRADE UNIONS AND A MINIMUM WAGE

It is extraordinary that we still subsidise employers who pay poverty wages and even more extraordinary that it has taken the Labour Party almost a century to move towards the concept of a statutory minimum wage. One of the reasons why we have taken so long is the fears which have been felt about the effect a statutory minimum wage would have on collective bargaining. The idea that we have to choose one or the other is simply wrong. Indeed, for an effective fair wages strategy we have to choose both. The Trade Unions have to organise the low paid against a background of legislative support which the Trade Unions themselves employ in the interests of their members. The Trade Unions will participate – through the processes of the National Economic Assessment – in determining the level of the minimum wage. They will be responsible for its enforcement. They will also have the duty of making sure that it is effective – that it amounts to more than the same levels of absolute and relative poverty at a higher level of inflation. I have no doubt that the Trade Unions will want to discharge all those tasks.

The hard fact is that collective bargaining will not and cannot, alone, end poverty wages. In some sections of private industry, Unions face insurmountable difficulties in reaching and enforcing collective agreements. In these unorganised sectors even recruitment is difficult. There is a high turnover of eligible employees – many of them seasonal or part time workers. Indeed 4 million of the 8 million low paid are part time women. Often potential Union members are organised in small units in highly inaccessible areas. As a result only one in six workers in private services were organised in Unions – even in the late 1970s, the high point of Union membership. In the catering industry, only 6 per cent of workers were Trade Union members.

Statutory support for minimum wage levels is just as consistent with collective bargaining as are health and safety regulations, employment protection legislation or equal opportunities standards. Union action – in all these fields – is only fully effective when augmented by the law. In the field of pay the Trade Unions have supported and defended the wages councils. The need for the Unions and the law to work in partnership in the achievement of living wage is accepted as obvious in other countries, where minimum wage legislation is now taken for granted – Australia, Canada, New Zealand, France, Holland, Belgium, Spain, Portugal and the United States of America.

THE PRACTICALITIES OF A MINIMUM WAGE

Those of us who support the introduction of a statutory minimum wage do our cause no favour by pretending that its implementation will be easy or without some penalties. The penalties should not be overstated. But if we are serious in our intention, it is much better to face and overcome them now than to be confounded by them when the policy is implemented. A national minimum wage has to be phased into our wage structure with some care. The joint Labour Party/TUC document is absolutely explicit about both the care and the phasing. No responsible party – and no responsible Trade Union movement – could make an exact commitment on either the level or timing of a national minimum wage before a general election. *Fair Wages Strategy* [TUC/Labour Party, April 1986] is explicit: 'The Labour Government will clearly wish to advance towards our longer-term goal of raising the legal minimum towards some generally accepted level of decency.' I am equally explicit. The next Labour Government will *begin* that advance immediately.

Of course, the introduction of a national minimum wage will be augmented by the re-introduction of the Fair Wages Resolution and an end to the privatisation of local authority and health service supplementary activities – both of which have resulted in a lower level of provision and an even lower level of wages for those who provide the new minimum facilities. But the Labour Government's initiative has to be reinforced by the Trades Unions themselves. Trade Union help is vital if the introduction of a national minimum wage is to be accomplished with minimum disturbance. But the Trades Unions also have a positive role. That role many Unions accept already. Bargaining with the specific intention of improving both the relative and absolute earnings of the low paid grows increasingly common. We need to see a greater emphasis on flat rate increases, improvements in basic pay (as distinct from plus elements), the use of minimum earnings levels, abolition of the lowest grades and the shortening of incremental scales. That is already the case in some sectors. A restructuring of pay in favour of lower grades has been carried out on behalf of NHS ancillaries and local authority manuals; the industrial Civil Service has restructured pay to eliminate lowest paid grades; and Unions in the chemicals industry are seeking extension of industry-wide agreements to cover cleaning and catering staff. Assuming that employers know how much they can afford in any one wage negotiation, if the Unions argue for a redistribution pattern which favours the lowest paid, the result not only moves towards the national minimum it does so in a way which makes no unacceptable addition to the cost of production. The Unions which negotiate with the conscious intention of improving the relative position of the low paid are implicitly recognising that it makes no sense to increase the wages at the bottom of the scale and push up the rest by equal proportions. That principle has to be extended into negotiations towards the national minimum wage.

Some critics of a national minimum wage fear that it is either an alternative to Trade Union negotiation or even a Trojan Horse which, once it has been wheeled into the industrial scene, will be opened to reveal an incomes policy. I therefore stress that far from superseding Union activity, the successful introduction of a national minimum wage is wholly dependent upon it. I also make clear that I am personally in favour of a statutory minimum wage and personally opposed to statutory incomes policy. Such a policy is not on the agenda of the next Labour Government. That is not to say that some agreement on the total increase in money wages is not necessary, if we are to achieve our goals of reducing unemployment by one million in two years. But that will be necessary – and its achievement will be discussed as part of the National Economic Assessment – whether or not we have a Fair Wages Strategy.

Without such a policy this country incurs economic as well as social penalties. Bad employers – with out-of-date machinery and even more archaic attitudes – will undercut the good. The introduction of new technology will be slowed down. And low wages will provide no guarantee of permanent employment. Low wages cannot compensate for the failure to invest and innovate. Winston Churchill eloquently put the case for statutory support for wages minima when he spoke in favour of the establishment of Wage Councils in 1909:

> It is a serious national evil that any class of His Majesty's subjects should receive less than a living wage in return for their utmost exertions. It was formerly supposed that the working of the laws of supply and demand would naturally regulate or eliminate that evil . . . But when you have no organisation, no parity of bargaining, the good employer is undercut by the bad and the bad employer is undercut by the worst [*Hansard*, Col. 388, vol. 4, 28 April 1909].

15 Britain, the Third World and the Debt Crisis*

THIRD WORLD NEWS

For a while, Band Aid and Sport Aid pushed the subject of the Third World to the top of the political agenda. Millions of men and women were inspired into working and contributing towards help for the starving people of the world. Unfortunately the great wave of moral indignation washed by the major Western governments. For all the benefits that the several Geldof initiatives provided, when set against the whole problem of global hunger they will only have a marginal effect. They should have stirred the world's conscience, set the pace and begun a new era of help and assistance. But the reality is quite the opposite. In 1985 alone the net transfer of resources from the Third to the Developed World was £22 billion. The truth is that the poorest parts of the world are still subsidising the richest.

Part of the problem is that 'the News' only tells us what is new in the Third World. It tells us about new tragedies, new disasters, new events. The Bhopal disaster in India killed three thousand people and was on the television screens and front pages of the newspapers world-wide. The fact that many more people in India will die of hunger and hunger-related diseases every year is such an old story that nobody bothers to report it.

It is the same with other sudden disasters, such as the Ethiopian famine. They only make 'the News' and elicit a response once they have occurred. Warnings in 1983 that a famine was building up in Ethiopia barely warranted a mention and certainly evoked no policy response.

But even when Third World crises do make 'the News' – the international debt crisis, for instance – the story is told in terms of how it affects us in the West. US and European banks teetering on the brink of insolvency and the disruption this might cause the

* Based on speech at World Development Movement Conference, Westminster, 22 September 1984; speech to Labour Aid and Development Committee, County Hall, London, 17 January 1985; speech to Overseas Development Institute, London, 10 June 1986.

Western financial system seemed of far more concern than the impact on the debtor nations. Indeed, when the LDCs did get a mention it was concerned with whether or not they would accept IMF imposed austerity programmes, rather than the poverty and disruption of production that is the inevitable counterpart of IMF intervention.

Labour – indeed Western World – policy should aim to do two things. First, it should be concerned with helping prevent those disasters, those famines, those tragedies that become so newsworthy once they occur. But second, it must be concerned with those issues that fail altogether to make 'the News' in the West.

Before I outline a number of policy steps which need to be taken, I think it is necessary to have some analysis of the problems at hand, for if we are to move beyond famine we must first understand what lies at its root.

ENTITLEMENTS

If we begin with the people at the bottom of the pile – the 500 million people who suffer chronic malnutrition – then their problem is their lack of what has been broadly termed 'entitlements'. They are not entitled to health care, or to education or even to the means of subsistence itself – food. Rather than being largely in control of their environment these people are subject to its vagaries – the weather, disease and natural disasters. This is not because it is beyond the wit of humankind to cope with, anticipate and plan for such problems. It is because the people affected normally live in such poverty that they are always vulnerable in a way that people in developed countries or even the élites within the LDCs are not.

The problems of these 'absolute poor' – the kind of people who populate much of Ethiopia and the Sub-Sahara, and increasingly the people who populate those intermediately developed countries which are subject to IMF programmes, such as Brazil – do not stem from a shortage of food or from the absence of remedies for the diseases many of them suffer. Their problems stem from lack of access or entitlement to the resources that are available.

There is no shortage of food world-wide. Indeed, the EEC

countries spend vast quantities of money either storing or destroying unused food. But even those countries with many starving people often do not suffer from either a shortage of food or a shortage of land suitable for food production. Brazil is one of the world's largest food exporters, and yet some areas report 25 per cent infant mortality, whilst one survey found that 70 per cent of the population of North East Brazil are malnourished. Guinea Bissau even banned the sale of peanuts to its local population in order to boost exports despite the fact that they are part of the staple diet of people in that country. In the Bangladesh famine of 1974 a very large number of people died in a year when food availability per head was at a peak – higher than any other year between 1971 and 1975.

Such apparent anomalies are, in fact, the norm in much of the less developed world. In the cases of Brazil and Guinea Bissau domestic consumption and imports have had to be savagely cut back whilst exports are promoted or substituted in order to service debts to Western banks or international lending institutions. The Third World as a whole generates an enormous surplus of money which then flows to the rich world. The sad irony is that much of the borrowing that built up these debts financed a development strategy that either failed to trickle down to the poorest people or in many cases actually increased the poverty and vulnerability of the worst off. Sadly the converse is not true, for it is the poorest who suffer most from the redoubled export efforts of the debtor governments.

In the case of disasters, such as the Ethiopian or Bangladeshi famines, incompetence, corruption, inadequate transport systems for the distribution of food and emergency relief, Governments that expropriate food to sell to bolster their revenues, the urban areas and the army all play a part in the scale of starvation and death that occur, but ultimately the reason the world's poorest suffer and die is that they have neither the economic nor the political capital to give a command over the resources that are available.

Given limited resources, there are three possible starting points for policy emphasis:

(a) Balance of payments adjustment.
(b) The promotion of growth.
(c) To stop people dying.

Where these three conflict – and they often do – then, unlike the current emphasis on balance of payments adjustment and growth, I think there is a moral duty to concentrate on the third problem. And this requires us to ask who is dying and why.

FOOD AID

I am not advocating that all aid and international credit be devoted to disaster relief or food aid. On the contrary, I am concerned with trying to direct resources to the alleviation of the poverty that both leads directly to disaster and prevents an adequate response to disasters once they have occurred. Indeed, except when it is used as emergency relief and adequate provision is made for its distribution, food aid often has dire consequences for the very people it is meant to help. Usually it is a means to dump Western food surpluses on the Third World, with the result that it undermines local food production and makes it even more difficult for indigenous farmers to scratch out a living. Worse still, much of the production for export by the Third World often takes up the best land and substitutes for local food production. It is used as an input for Western farmers. For instance, in the Guinea Bissau example I quoted earlier, most of the peanuts that local people are forbidden from purchasing end up as foodstuffs for European cows or pigs. Some of the surplus milk products produced by the cows is then sent back to Africa as food aid.

DOES DEVELOPMENT ASSISTANCE TRICKLE DOWN?

Perhaps one of the problems of the policies of both individual Western governments as well as the international agencies is their tendency to look at any particular country as a whole rather than at the needs of the most vulnerable groups within a country. If the problem is perceived to be a lack of food then this may encourage a policy of what is sometimes termed 'accelerated development' whereby aid is focused on the more fertile areas and on those classes of people such as the richer peasants, that have the most potential to increase their own production. Moreover, if the aid is based on credit it is only the richer areas or peasants that can provide the collateral to attract the loans. The poorest subsistence farmers, who have much less potential to export productions and no collateral for borrowing to finance improvements, receive no help. The net effect is that their production cannot compete. Their land is purchased from them and they become landless labourers. The result is that with little or no income they have no entitlement to or command over the extra food that is produced. Indeed, that purchasing power may be so feeble that it is more profitable to produce cash crops such as coffee, cotton, tobacco or the like for export than to produce crops for domestic consumption.

Leaving the question of the profitability of export crops aside, exports may be encouraged in order to generate funds for the purchase of imports of the technologies necessary to help the development of industry or perhaps the Western consumption patterns of the wealthier classes. More recently, they have been used to meet debt repayments.

A concentration on exports can provide quite a high rate of *per capita* growth without ever filtering down to the poorest – indeed it may even worsen their plight.

In short, growth and development are not necessarily the same thing. In the case of IMF adjustment programmes we may even get decline rather than growth. Domestic demand and government spending including development programmes are cut back in order to reduce imports and generate the largest surplus for the repayment of debt. When a number of countries pursue such a strategy simultaneously they simply undermine exports to each other and deepen the depression. IMF policies are only really designed to help bring about short-run adjustment in a small number of countries on the assumption that other countries continue to grow. Once they are applied almost universally, they are disastrous, exacerbating the problems of each individual country and providing a long-term solution in none.

WHICH GROWTH STRATEGY?

Moreover, export-led growth or export-led debt repayment programmes tend to create their own problems, particularly when pursued by a whole host of LDCs simultaneously. Just as with IMF imposed deflation and cuts in imports the sum of the parts undermines the whole. Commodity prices are forced down by over-production so that the West is able to enjoy the lowest commodity prices for fifty years and ease its inflation. Since 1980 there has been a 21 per cent decrease in commodity prices in general, a 25 per cent drop in non-food agricultural prices for items such as cotton and wool and a 35 per cent drop in metal prices. Food prices have been hit by EEC over-production as a result of CAP and other prices by substitution such as the replacement of metals by plastics in cars. LDCs have tried to rebuild their earnings by producing ever more for export thus forcing down prices ever lower. In some cases money spent on expanding the production of export crops would earn a better return if it was simply deposited in a Western bank. Where the LDCs do succeed in producing either crops or manufactures, which compete with, rather than complement, production in the West they are usually hampered by comprehensive systems of tariffs such as the Multi Fibre agreement or the CAP.

If the Labour Party enters the next election still in favour of a system of import controls then it must bear in mind two facts. First, the most rapid penetration has been achieved by industrial goods from other developed countries, not those from the LDCs. Second, it is often the industrial products of the LDCs that are first to suffer from restrictions on trade. Any system of import controls would have to take account of this.

Although the encouragement and development of the industrial sector of LDCs may often lead to uneven development and the growth of urban unemployment and rural depopulation, trade and aid policy pointed in this direction may have a less debilitating effect on the poor than concentration on the production of primary products and cash crops. The development of the industrial sector may also lay a more satisfactory foundation for long-term growth. Too much reliance on primary produce leaves a country far more subject to the swings of commodity prices and can lead to patterns of production that both prove unsuitable and increase starvation.

When we discuss policy towards the very poorest alongside industrialisation policy, we soon see the impossibility of devising a single policy stance towards the Third World. The LDCs are not a homogeneous group of countries. They are at different stages of development and different development strategies are appropriate for different countries. Thus whilst our first priority must be the very poorest, this does not necessarily always conflict with the needs of the intermediately developed countries who should also be taken account of in our trade policies and in the policies we promote in the international institutions.

THE INTERNATIONAL DEBT CRISIS

The international debt crisis has now dragged on for so long that some commentators have begun to argue that it is not a crisis at all. The international banking system tottered but it survived. The strategy which averted the outright default of the debtor nations was specifically endorsed by the 1984 London Summit which concluded that it 'should continue to enable the international financial system to manage any problems which may still arise'. The commercial banks of Europe and America are said to have saved themselves and vindicated the system. For that to be true, the system has to be defined as one which has neither care nor compassion for the developing world.

For the worst effects of the debt crisis were not on the banking system but on the people of the Third World; and for them the crisis persists. It was, in part, created by the way in which the commercial banks sought to obtain huge profits from international loans. It was intensified by the way those banks sought to protect their lending after the debtor nations moved towards complete insolvency as a result of the world recession which the Governments of the West exacerbated as a solution to their endemic inflation.

The crisis began with the first oil shock of the 1970s, which resulted in non-oil producing countries being squeezed by mounting oil bills and the collapse of their export markets in industrial countries. Some of the developing countries were spending 60 per cent of their export earnings on oil alone. The oil price increase impaired the ability of Third World countries to repay, or even service, their debts. The basic failure in the system was the privatisation of international finance. When the two oil shocks of the 1970s produced the giant increase in financial flows which largely originated in the OPEC countries they should have been channelled through the official institutions. Instead the rescue operations were left to the private banks in London and New York who made high, if erratic, profits on recycling the money to Third World countries at interest rates which reflected nothing except a determination to receive the largest return possible. The banks paid little or no attention to the economic health of their clients.

The reaction of the developed world to the crisis made servicing and repayment almost impossible. Western Europe and North America responded to the oil price increase by deepening their incipient deflation. The cost of borrowing escalated as the developed nations attempted to squeeze inflation out of their economies. Demand fell and the markets for many Third World exports collapsed. Commodity prices slumped to their lowest level since the Second World War – falling by as much as 15 per cent in a single year. In the monetarist economies of the West, aid was cut as a contribution to the reduction in public expenditure which was seen as an essential ingredient in the prescription for recovery. Debtor nations became literally incapable of fulfilling their commitments.

At first, the commercial banks arranged the rescheduling of outstanding debt but when Mexico seemed likely to default on a debt that totalled 80 billion dollars, the whole international banking system seemed to be at risk, so the Reagan administration, the Bank of International Settlement and the International Monetary Fund mounted concerted action 'to ensure continued smooth functioning of the international financial system'. The effect of the rescue package on Mexico was left for President Lopez Portillo to describe in his valedictory speech: 'They looted us . . . They will not loot us again'. He was at least half right, and he might have added that Lloyds, Citibank, Chase Manhattan, Midland and Bank of America, all made huge profits out of relatively poor countries whilst contributing little to their long-term development.

The accepted wisdom of the West is that the problems of debtor nations must be seen individually as the difficulties arise from imprudence and over-spending. The 1984 London Summit specifically ruled out any strategy for assisting them in achieving the national income growth which is necessary if they are to meet their debt. Instead salvation was seen as coming from a series of exercises in international money lending with the borrowers being invited to choose between the lenders' terms and bankruptcy. The Prime Minister adopts what she, no doubt, regards as a moralistic view. The Third World has a duty to its bankers and should tighten its belt and pay off its overdraft.

To return to solvency through rescheduled loans negotiated with the commercial banks, the debtor nations have been forced to obtain the IMF's approval for their domestic economic policy. That support has only been provided after the introduction of policies which deepen recession, weaken trade and, therefore, in the long term, reduce ability to pay. The IMF demands deflation, cuts in government spending and a generally diminished level of economic activity. All these demands stifle growth. Yet growth is the only possible long-term remedy for the debt crisis.

BRITAIN'S POLICY TOWARDS THE THIRD WORLD

Nobody believes or suggests that the Government of a medium sized country could solve, on its own, any of the international crises which we face. But we could have a crucial influence on their solution. Taking the example of the international debt crisis, Great Britain is a member of, or represented in, all the institutions which determine international finance policy – the World Bank, the IMF, the Group of Five, the Commonwealth, the United Nations and the EEC. We also speak with special authority in these matters because of the role in international finance played by the City. In many cases we would be able to tip the balance in the direction of a more economically sensible as well as morally acceptable policy. In all cases we should be advocating such policies. The problem of the less developed world will only be solved multinationally. We ought to be arguing for those solutions and, in the meantime, doing what we can whenever an individual opportunity to help arises. The policy decisions which we have to face come under four headings:

1. Co-ordination and Reflation.
2. Debt Management.
3. Aid.
4. The Banking System.

CO-ORDINATION AND REFLATION

The extent to which the UK can expand is clearly constrained by the fiscal stance taken by other major industrial nations. We will find it easier to meet our unemployment targets if there is co-ordinated international expansion. That co-ordinated expansion is vital if we are to create the environment in which the Third World can meet its debt obligation. To that end, the parties of the Socialist International are committed to a co-ordinated expansion programme.

The British Government must put pressure on the IMF to modify its 'country by country' approach. Clearly account has to be taken of the different problems faced by different countries. But solutions applied to, and imposed by, one country must not intensify the difficulties of another. The idea that each of the debtor nations can simultaneously – yet individually – meet their debts through the imposition of an austerity package is morally indefensible and economically illiterate. It requires the poor of the Third World to suffer and die in order to service and repay debts from which they did not benefit and which they had no part in negotiating. And austerity programmes, which were introduced as a temporary measure, cannot be a permanent solution – particularly in the new conditions of slower growth, higher world interest rates and attempts to reduce imports even in the creditor nations. The debt crisis cannot be solved by short-term measures, and it is foolish of the IMF to pretend otherwise.

A combined response – including co-ordinated reflation – is essential to the interests of both the developing and industrially developed world. It is the only way to combat the growing call for protectionism within the United States. A European reflation is the only way to combat the reduction in international economic activity which would follow a reduction in the American deficit.

DEBT MANAGEMENT

The Socialist International has set out five policies which the West should adopt to ease the burden of debt. Those policies a Labour Government will seek to have implemented by the West:

– Conversion of the debts of poorer countries into grants. That is particularly important for the countries of sub-Saharan Africa. We must also convert into grants part of the debt of other developing countries.
– Rescheduling of the remaining debt of Third World countries,

through extension of the time period for repayment of principal; with particular reference to those Latin American countries whose scale of current indebtedness not only limits their import capacity, but also threatens the security of financial institutions in First World countries.

- A ceiling on interest rates at concessionary levels for developing countries. Such measures would complement extending the time period for repayment of principal and lowered interest rates.
- An increase of Special Drawing Rights over a five-year period, to a US dollar equivalent of approximately 150 billion to support the process of debt readjustment, recovery and development.
- A fixing of the ratio of debt repayment to a given proportion of developing countries' export earnings, at a maximum of 20 per cent, which was typical in the early 1970s. Such a measure again would complement extending the time period for repayment of principle and lowered interest rates.

AID

On the subject of aid, the Socialist International is equally explicit. The Labour Party contributed to those decisions. In Government we shall support their implementation:

- Increasing official development assistance to the 0.7 per cent of GDP recommended by the Brandt Commission and the United Nations. If this were achieved, and if those countries already exceeding 0.7 per cent were to sustain their exceptional contribution, it would not only amount to a significant increase in the resources of the South, but also create an additional two million jobs in the OECD countries of the North.
- A complementary increase in the funds of IDA or – pending a change in the willingness of the US administration to contribute to the replenishment of IDA funds – action by other countries in the North to provide adequate finance for parallel World Bank initiatives, such as the proposed Fund for Africa.

Whilst we must accept that the debt crisis causes us to increase the total amount of aid we make available, it is important to ensure that the increase does not, in itself, distort the programme. Aid must not be diverted into debt relief and thus used to help large borrowers at the expense of smaller borrowers with greater needs and superior policies. Aid must not be used to conceal debt incurred in the pursuit of politically unacceptable policies. Aid must not contribute to a further build up of financial obligations which produce a new debt crisis.

THE BANKING SYSTEM

The burden that international debt currently imposes on the international economic system has strong parallels with the drag that German reparations imposed on the inter-war economy in Europe. Even if we examine the result in the hard language of self-interest the risks are clear. It is at least possible that the problem of debt will be 'solved' by the default of a major borrower – for example Mexico – just as the drag imposed by reparations in the 1920s and 1930s was 'dealt with' by the default of Germany.

Indeed it has been fears for the banking system of the West rather than fears for the living standards of the South that has prompted most concern amongst the bankers and government of the Developed World.

In practice the burden of default will have to be spread between the defaulter, the stockholders of the banks concerned and the Western tax payer. At first sight it may appear unreasonable that the tax payer should meet the bill for the incompetence of the private sector – but were the worst to happen, the cost would certainly have to be met by the Government. The consequences of a major clearing bank collapse in the UK would be so catastrophic that there would be no alternative to public intervention.

However, the stockholders of the private banks who grew rich on the easy pickings of Third World loans in the 1970s will also have to pay a price. In particular it is only reasonable that, if the tax payer is to shoulder the burden of private sector debt, the contribution should be matched by the acquisition of equity in the bank concerned. Of course, the equity should carry with it corresponding public representation at board level.

The potential threat imposed by default may also require us to review the adequacy of the mechanisms protecting UK depositors and to consider introducing a scheme similar to the American Federal Deposit Insurance scheme.

The problem for the West in the future is to ensure that additional flows of resources to the Third World are not wasted. It is certainly correct to blame the Western banks for their greedy response to the prospect of high and easy returns from the Third World and their inadequate project appraisal of the real risks. But they are certainly not the only culprits. Much of the blame lies with circumstances beyond their control – falling oil and commodity prices, the recession of the 1980s, energy conservation, tight monetary policies and high interest rates pursued by Western Governments. And we must also recognise the blame that attaches to some of the less developed countries themselves – domestic corruption, excessive arms expenditure, incompetent Government and the substitution of cash crops for subsistence production are just some of the problems there.

THE BAKER PLANS

The plans put forward by James Baker in the US are inadequate and in some cases misguided, but they should not be entirely dismissed. It is the first time that one of the major countries of the world has acknowledged that a co-ordinated response to the debt crisis is required and as a result complete reliance on *laissez-faire* has at last been jettisoned. At least Baker recognised that the US dollar and interest rates could only be brought down by international co-operation. And he also recognises the need for the co-ordination of fiscal policy and an increase in the flow of financial support to the less developed countries. However, the Baker plans rely on the use of country by country austerity packages and involve a naive faith in free market forces and the supposed benefits that cuts in Third World public sector will bring. They are also designed to open up the LDCs to give freer access to American exports and American multinational companies.

For all their shortcomings we must hope that the Baker plans signal a shift in the world political environment back towards more co-operation. For it is only in such an environment that most of the policies we advocate for the less developed world have any chance of implementation or success.